AF632989

Glimpses of Comparative Literature

Glimpses of Comparative Literature

Edited by

Ram Prakash Pradhan

ATLANTIC

PUBLISHERS & DISTRIBUTORS (P) LTD

Published by
ATLANTIC
PUBLISHERS & DISTRIBUTORS (P) LTD
7/22, Ansari Road, Darya Ganj,
New Delhi-110002
Phones : +91-11-40775252, 23273880, 23275880, 23280451
Fax : +91-11-23285873
Web : www.atlanticbooks.com
E-mail : orders@atlanticbooks.com

Branch Office
5, Nallathambi Street, Wallajah Road,
Chennai-600002
Phones : +91-44-64611085, 32413319
E-mail : chennai@atlanticbooks.com

© 2011 Ram Prakash Pradhan for selection and editorial matter; the contributors for individual chapters.

ISBN 978-81-269-1634-4

All rights reserved. No part of this publication may be reproduced, stored in a retrieval system, transmitted or utilized in any form or by any means, electronic, mechanical, photocopying, recording or otherwise, without the prior permission of the copyright owner. Application for such permission should be addressed to the publisher.

Printed in India at Nice Printing Press, A-33/3A, Site-IV, Industrial Area, Sahibabad, Ghaziabad, U.P.

Dedicated to

My sons

Yash and Harsh

PREFACE

Comparative study of literature in the same language or in different languages through translation seems imperative today as it contributes to critical scholarship and revaluation of literature. Its multilingual range widens the horizons of the readers' knowledge and also helps them in exploring the relative merits of one work in the light of the other. Critics like Arnold also prescribed the comparative method for discovering the nerve of literature. Such step may break the national boundary of the alienation of literature and may open universal dimension for its de-alienation. It is in such context that the fourteen articles in this volume are intended for perusal and better understanding of literature so that one may enjoy the universal state of intercommunion of literature.

The similarity of theme in *The Inheritance of Loss* and *Home* exposes lines of hypocrisy in matters of sex and romance and conveys without reservation the message that the females are not always so much at fault as they are taken to be. The comparative study of Amitav Ghosh's *The Hungry Tide* and Kiran Desai's *The Inheritance of Loss* shows that Ghosh achieves superb literary effect in his work while Desai disappoints the reader with her synthetic approach towards the major issues. The celebration of Black Motherhood in Gloria Naylor's *The Women of Brewster Place* and in Toni Morrison's *The Bluest Eye* is a vibrant portrait of what a mother is and what the act of mothering should be. Such glorification of motherliness is protective of Black women in their fight against white racism.

The paper on Rushdie and Naipaul explores how far these two writers can be considered to be examples for the young English writers in India. They are the product of western system and address an audience that is primarily western. They ignore Indian literary traditions and hence to get an inspiration from them for Indian writing in English is to knock at the wrong doors. The study of *The Namesake* and *The Inheritance of Loss* highlights the idea how diasporic space of Kiran Desai is very broad as it is related to a number of issues like globalization, economic inequality, multiculturalism, immigration, racism and terrorism while Lahiri is mainly concerned with the problems of the Bengali immigrants in America. Both writers belong to the second generation of diasporic writing and both have contributed to the growth of fiction writing.

What the Body Remembers and *Difficult Daughters*, the two novels of Shauna Singh Baldwin and Manju Kapur respectively, have in common the 1947 partition of the subcontinent as their main theme and portray the victimization of women in human society. The former illustrates the social matrix and milieu whereas the latter heralds the change towards a progressive society. The comparative study of Indian poetics and the concepts of Greek drama presents both of them as poles apart. Indian plays never leave any painful impression upon the audience whereas the structure of Greek drama has an essential feature of tragic conflict in it.

Voice of protest in *Untouchable* is more vocal and revolutionary than that in *Choma's Drum*. The circumstances of both the untouchables, Bakha and Choma appear to be different but the fundamental issue is one and the same—how to maintain one's identity in an orthodoxical racist society. Hence, the comparative study is much revealing.

The paper "The Child in Modern Indian Fiction: A Comparative Study of Two Indian Novels" attempts to make a comparative study of the representation of the child in a couple of modern Indian novels written in two different languages. Children have been made protagonists and the entire issue of the representation of the child in Indian fiction in postcolonial context deserves critical attention. Ontology of language is studied with reference to Tagore's *Gitanjali* and Paul de Man's theory of rhetorical reading. Paul de Man has been the most rigorous practitioner of deconstructive readings. The author of the paper brings home the point that deconstruction may disturb western metaphysics but in the eastern philosophy it had been experienced long back since the time of the Vedas. *Gitanjali* is a perfect example of naming the void between the sign and the meaning.

The comparative study of "Whitman, Eliot, and the *Bhagavadgita*" is comprehensive and delightful as it reveals how the two most important American poets with their large followers and widespread influences have been influenced by the *Bhagavadgita*, the epitome of Indian philosophy and religion. The critic concludes how Whitman has got the right spirit of the *Gita* while Eliot's poetry, in spite of several references to the Indian scriptures, shows a clear dichotomy between the divine and physical world which goes against the spirit of the *Gita*.

Two major texts of two different languages English and Hindi have been studied with reference to *Nectar in a Sieve* and *Godan.* Both the novels deal with rural life and the problems of tenant farmers. While Premchand is the son of the soil, Kamala Markandaya is considered as a diasporic and anglicized writer so far as her knowledge of rural life is concerned.

Conrad's *Heart of Darkness* is the product of an imperialist culture while Achebe's *Things Fall Apart* is a product of the hybrid culture born of the fusion of colonial European and indigenous African cultures. Achebe's novel represents the African experience and is different from the colonial novel in its structure, language and perspective.

The tragic ethos of Pecola and Tess is basically the same in spite of the fact that one is victim of the rising industrial culture and the other is a prey to racist factor under white domination of America. The literary device of comparing notes contributes to better illustration of the thematic issue of the writer.

The book will prove useful to the students and teachers of English Literature and researchers in this field.

Ram Prakash Pradhan

ACKNOWLEDGEMENTS

I take this opportunity to thank all those people who have directly or indirectly helped me in bringing out this book in such a nice form. I am particularly grateful to all the contributors who have worked hard to present their well-researched papers. I am extremely thankful to Prof. R.N. Rai for his constant encouragement to complete the book. I am deeply indebted to my father Dr. Ram Prasiddh Pradhan, former Reader & Head, Dept. of English, P.G. College, Ghazipur, who has been a source of academic inspiration to me. My mother Smt. Champa Rai's motivation enabled me to accomplish the task. I acknowledge with thanks my wife Chandralekha Rai's cooperation, encouragement and concern ceaselessly shown during the period of my editing this book. I also appreciate the cooperation of my sons—Yash and Harsh. Special thanks are also due to my younger brother Ravi Prakash Pradhan and his wife Tanu Rai.

Ram Prakash Pradhan

Contents

1

Kiran Desai's *The Inheritance of Loss* and Manju Kapur's *Home*: A Similarity of Theme

Satendra Kumar

The present article is a holistic venture and modest attempt to decipher at hatching the graph of the lives of hypocrisy through the characters depicted in the novels in order to embark upon the similarity of theme in the novels of Manju Kapur's *Home* and Kiran Desai's *The Inheritance of Loss*. Indubitably both Kapur and Desai are the rising stars in the firmament of Indo-English Literature. Both of them have had the current theme in their novels with aplomb success and triumph. Both of them have the charismatic and talented personalities—one based in Delhi and the other in America and pleased the readers with their honeyed expression. Newcomer Kiran Desai, who is currently a student in Columbia University's creative writing course, was born in India in 1971 and educated in India, England and the United States, is the daughter of highly praised Indian novelist, Anita Desai. Kiran Desai was fifteen when she left India—she lived in England for a year and has been in the US since then—and it's tempting to pigeonhole her as another NRI writer obsessed by themes like dislocation (something that certainly runs through *Inheritance*).

Kiran Desai has written two novels *Hullabaloo in the Guava Orchard* and *The Inheritance of Loss*. At the age of 35, she became the youngest woman ever to win Britain's Man

Booker Prize, for her novel *The Inheritance of Loss*—a career-stirring event for any budding novelist, but particularly so in her case, because it is an honour that has eluded her celebrated mother, Anita Desai, who has been a finalist three times for the prize. The novel is based partly on her family history, in her mother's house in Cold Spring, New York, in "a completely happy atmosphere of stillness and peace", she said, speaking in a soft, Anglo-Indian lilt. "The light in her house seems golden." Mother and daughter worked side-by-side on their separate manuscripts during the day, then cooked together at night, Desai said, and drank rum. When she finished the first draft of "Inheritance", "it was an enormous mess", Desai said. She showed it to her mother. "She was terrified and I was terrified."

Manju Kapur, who also authored *Difficult Daughters* and *A Married Woman*, writer and Professor of English at Miranda House in Delhi University, insists that the world she creates in her novels is not because of any personal analysis of the world in front of her. It stems the intellectual experience of her academic life. "I can analyze only because I am a teacher", revealed in one of the interviews.[1] The novelist started writing this novel in 1994 and would have been her first novel, had she not got stuck and moved on to *Difficult Daughters* instead. Having started her writing career late her 40s—middle-age angst had something to do with it—she realizes she cannot afford to "take forever" on one book. She is happy as she is passing her moment between college, home and writing. "Writers are not stars. They are not public figures", she believes. That makes two things she does not have in common with Rushdie. In one of the interviews she unlocks, "I get both inspired and depressed. I wish I could write like that. Writing is a muscle that needs to be exercised all the time."[2]

Putting on the anvil for test and striking criticality with hammer I find that both the female novelists have had the treatment of romance and sex equally and acutely, minutely and sharply as if they might have had the same experience in their lives. Kapur's superb novel *Home* is filled with the examples of romance—vulgar, refined and virginal, and sex.

Banwari Lal—a man of high principles and some passion, of unswerving moral and physical courage, of genuine affection and great tenderness, of honest pride and sturdy independence, and of strong commonsense, patriarch of a cloth business in the middle class New Delhi neighbourhood of Karol Bagh, is a believer in the old ways. Men work out of the home, women within.[3] Men carry forward the family line, women enable their mission.[4] His two sons unquestioningly follow their father in business and life, but their wives will not. Neither will his granddaughter, who makes choices considered unavoidable to the women of the family.[5]

The eldest son Yashpal got married with Sona and the novelist snatched the situation dipped in romance:

> Her husband looked at her with approval. 'You are my everything,' he murmured into her ear. His parents in the next room were sleeping, he could now lock his door, now undress his wife, still shy. With the lights off, he at last got what he had longed for all day. (10)
>
> Yashpal's love was so overwhelming that he was driven to demonstrate it endlessly. In the way his eyes kept seeking her face, in the small gifts he secretly gave, in the way he waited for her to finish eating before leaving the dinning area, in the way he hung around the kitchen when she was cooking, in the way he demanded her presence even when he was talking to his mother. (10-11)

In yet another romantic situation, Yashpal drew Sona soft and yielding to mass to himself. His arms around her, he tugged at her lower lip, sucking it. In the morning he knew it would look even redder and only he would know the reason. This secret made him increase the pressure. Sona's hand crept to his pyjama tape, the darkness allowed her to do things she never would have if they could see each other. She opened the buttons of her blouse, slithered down, kissing him all the way to finally press her breast on either side of his erection. Yashpal moaned. Sona took him in her mouth, teasing him with her tongue. The man arched into her, and thought no one on earth could ever be a wife to him but Sona and he would give his life to please her. They made a plan for tour and on the tour nightly away from home, family and shop; Yashpal gave himself over to the pleasure of his wife's body. Sona had not realized how much difference leisure and a change of location could make to a man's sex drive.

The second son Pyare Lal was also married with Sushila who brought a great dowry while the first one did not bring. By the time Pyare Lal was twenty-six he was the father of two sons. As the children grew, Vicky hovered uneasily between shop and home, between upstairs and downstairs, between his grandparents and his aunts. By the time, he was fifteen he was moody and gangly. He looked as though he had worms. In one of the hot situations and incidents Vicky (orphaned-son of Murli and Sunita, the only daughter of Lala Banwari Lal) and Nisha (daughter of Yashpal and Sona, the only granddaughter of Lala Banwari Lal) were found crossing the limit of the limitations:

> She (Nisha) threw herself on his back and put her arms around his neck. 'You have me, Vicky, you have me,' she said, rocking against his back, while Vicky sniveled into his sleeve. (56)
>
> Now she dug her puzzled chin into Vicky's back. How could one show anybody in her home? There were too many. They were not paying attention.
>
> '*Bas*. Now get off my back. You are getting heavy.' He put his hands around the plum legs, stroked them up and down, while trying to pull her off.
>
> Nisha wound her feet around his stomach. Vicky pulled her legs again and she slid around into his lap, laughing. Vicky looked at her. She was so sweet. If only she was his real sister he would not have to leave her one day.
>
> Nisha started resetting the upset snakes and ladders. 'Now you have to play with me. Before you run away.'
>
> 'You will have forgotten me,' said Vicky. He stretched himself beside Nisha, moodily rolling the dice. Gradually he curled himself around her, his head propped on one hand. She leant against him, her mind on the game. Her

dress rose higher as she fidgeted, her legs banging up and down on the durrie, next to Vicky's nose. Entranced, he put his hand on the inside of her beckoning thigh and whispered, 'How soft you are, Nisha.'

An intent look came on his face, his gentle fingers kept up a steady stroking. He began to trace the elastic of her panties all around the leg. 'What are you doing? *Chee*, that's dirty, take your hand away,' she cried, but Vicky was in no state to hear her. Panting slightly, he pushed his hand inside, touching the place where she did *su-su*, tracing the slit that divided her. Nisha wriggled even more frantically—'I'll tell everybody how dirty you are'—but his grip tightened and his arm pressed her thigh down so that both legs were parted and the slit was looser. A little *su-su* she could not help came out and wet his hand. She tried to draw her legs up and away from him but he forced himself closer.

'We are not going to tell anybody about this,' he whispered, holding her. 'This is our secret. See, you have done *su-su*. Ajay, Vijay and I are always doing *su-su* in front of each other.'

He put those fingers against his mouth. 'Give me your hand,' he went on. 'I want to show you something.'

'I don't want to see.' Nisha was crying.

'Of course you do.'

'No I want to go to Mummy. Leave me.'

'See, another secret.' And quickly, so quickly that she did not know how it happened, he introduced *it* to her. Terror-stricken, she looked at the black thing sticking up and down and then quickly looked away.

'Feel it.' He grabbed her hand. She pulled back and felt the stiff, straight thing knock against her fist. It felt dry and hard and hot.

'See.' Vicky's voice was hoarse. Once she started looking she couldn't look away. It appeared weird, repulsive and fascinating. 'Hold it, go on.'

> 'No, no I don't want to.'
>
> Vicky gripped her wrist so hard and painfully that her fingers opened around the big dark thing. There it was the small, pudgy, fair little hand against the much darker skin, with the boy's larger hand clamped over the girl's.
>
> He started moving their hands up and down. Quickly the tempo increased as the fear grew in her. When she tried to struggle, he increased the pressure of his hand.
>
> He gasped and out spurted white liquid on to the snakes and ladders, then trickled down her fist. The thing shrank, his face shriveled. 'It is our secret. If you tell anyone, they will beat you and me.' He gripped her arm. 'No one must ever know. No one. You understand.'
>
> Nisha nodded wordlessly. Vicky wiped her hand, then the snakes and ladders, with a corner of his shirt, and gave the game to her. She looked it gingerly. They started down, Vicky clutching the durrie and his books, his hair flying over his forehead, his blue Bata chappals going clutter-futter loudly down the stairs. Nisha followed. (57-59)

In another sexual and romantic incident Vicky got another opportunity to encounter with her:

> 'What are you doing?' Vicky asked.
>
> Nisha bent her head further over her book.
>
> There was a silence for a while. Then Vicky murmured, 'Nisha?'
>
> 'I'll tell Mummy you are not letting me study.'
>
> 'Mummy has gone upstairs with Raju.'
>
> 'Dadi then.'
>
> 'She is talking to the neighbor.'
>
> 'Go away.'
>
> He shifted a little closer. Instantly her skin began to prickle.
>
> 'Nisha,' he whispered,' 'are you angry with me?'
>
> The smallest shake of the head.

> 'Then why aren't you talking to me?'
>
> 'I'm talking to you.'
>
> 'Here,' he coaxed, drawing her stiff, resisting body nearer him, 'show me that you are not angry with me,' His hands reached under her dress. She pressed her thighs tightly together, but his fingers forced themselves between her legs. A little *su-su* she could not help came out and wet her panties. She wanted to die of shame.
>
> 'What have you done, naughty? So big and wetting your panties?' he said hoarsely, his lips against her ear. He started stroking her, the wet panty resting on the knobbly knuckle. 'See, I am drying you,' he rasped. 'You must thank me, dirty girl.'
>
> She tried shaking her head, bumping it against his shoulder, but he was concentrating on what he was doing and his grip grew harder. She winced in pain, his deep, uneven breaths against her cheek.
>
> In a daze she struggled against the body that was pressing itself so completely into her. Her book fell from her hand. She could feel him tugging at something behind her back. Then he reached around, took her hand, and clasped it on that hot monstrous thing. She turned away her head, he gripped the hand in his and began the fast movement up and down but not for long-liquid came, his clutch loosened, he sighed, moaned and wiped her hand.
>
> 'If you say anything to anybody,' muttered Vicky unnecessarily into her ear. 'They will beat you. They will lock you up, and never let you go to school.'
>
> Nisha freed herself, got up unsteadily and went into the *angan*. (62-63)

Similarly we could see the refined romance in the relation between Prem Nath and Rupa, sister of Sona:

> That evening, having dropped Nisha off at her mother's, Rupa returned home, had her bath and served her husband tea. 'Having children in a joint family is not easy,' she remarked.

Prem Nath looked at her. The days his wife visited her sister's house, she would return either depressed or withdrawn or with an air of tenderness that told him things were going badly with Sona. He now pulled her towards him and put his hands under her petticoat.

'Oho, what are you doing?'

'Why? There is no one here.'

'How can you be so shameless?'

'How can a man be shameless with his own wife? You want me to be shameless with some other woman?' he demanded.

'Chut,' scolded Rupa, playfully pushing away his hand, but sitting close so she was within arm's reach. She pulled the tray towards herself and started pouring tea.

Her husband looked admirably at her. There she was, hair still thick, and black, skin still smooth and young, dressing gown carelessly tied so he could see the large, heavy breasts swaying against the soft material with every movement she made. As she bent down to put tea on the little table next to him, his eye followed the way they swung out and down and then his hand followed his eye.

Rupa went on with her routine struggle. 'You are not listening about Raju ji,' she complained.

'I am,' said her husband, as he increased his caresses. He caught his wife's pouting lip between his own and sucked it. He massages her heavy buttocks towards him. Let's try *it* on a chair, he suggested, increased the pressure and spreading open her legs.

'I don't know where you get your ideas from,' said Rupa. 'Thank God no one knows what all you make me do.'

'Who else do I have in the world but you? God intended it like this.'

'Still'.

> 'No still. Why else did he not give us children? Otherwise you too would be dancing attendance on some Raju, day and night. Where would be the time or place to do anything?' asked the husband as he got up to lock the door.
>
> As the rhythms between them became faster on the chair, her husband pressed her straining body towards himself and whispered, 'Tell me, does your sister get this and this and this?' while she cried and told him stop, she didn't know and why should she care. But he went on because it excited him and he wanted her to know that her sister was not rich in everything, there were things to be had. 'Ask her,' he moaned and she moaned back that he was a shameless man. (100-01)

Nisha entered DBC with confidence. It was during the journey to the campus that Nisha really felt grown up. For the first time she was leaving the Karol Bagh alone. In the morning, she caught the University Special, the bus service that created to all the colleges, where girls and boys were not segregated, where the travellers were young. She first noticed his (Suresh) dark glasses and long hair. He was tall and thin, with a sallow complexion and his face was decorated with a bluish-black stubble. He took off his glasses to make sure she knew he was looking at her. She looked away, annoyed by his familiarity. It was their entrance in the romance which increased day to day and out and out. Her meetings with Suresh became regular. At coffee house one day he looked long and hard at her.

> 'What? asked the girl.
>
> 'Have you ever thought of cutting your hair?' he responded.
>
> 'My hair?' she repeated. This thing not her own, but the family treasure, the essence of traditional beauty, oiled all her life by loving hands, first vigorously to establish growth, then lightly to keep it tidy.
>
> You'll look really pretty. Like Suriya. You have eyes like her.'

> 'I don't know,' she faltered.
>
> 'If you could, you'd look like Suriya, I'm telling you,' he insisted (148). And one day he coaxed her for the hair cutting saloon.

They also frequently visited theatre for seeing the movie and the hit of the season was *Hum Aap Ke Hain Kaun*, the longest-running film after *Mother India*. In the dark film hall, Suresh had whispered she was as pretty as Madhuri Dixit. In the dark film hall she could respond to the pressure of his hand. Prettiness and love went together. It was there on the screen, it was there in her own home in the shape of her mother, whose beauty had moved her father to endure family disapproval (156). May be it will be like that with me, thought Nisha, swept by the magic of the songs and the appeal of the story. By this time Suresh's hands were all over her, she was slumped in her seat, her head heavy with desire, her heart pulpy with longing. During the interval, after a particular intimate session on seats where the dividing arm between them was only a notional barrier, Suresh would breathe, 'I love you, *yaar*.' On the way back in the scooter-rickshaw, they sat close together, thighs touching. Going to cinema became their favorite activity (157).

In another situation, the novelist snatched the occasion of romance when they took haven in a room of his friend:

> It was a corner house in the back lane of a gully. Suresh unlatched the door into angan without the sound. Some clothes were drying on cement banisters which led to a little room on top covered with corrugated sheets. They crept upstairs past the clothes, particularly crawling behind the balustrade, the steps were so high. At the top Suresh quietly struggled with the clanking lock.
>
> They were inside an airless, tiny room with peeling paint....
>
> He put his arms around her, pulling her closer than she had ever been. His smell rose pungent, male and musky. 'So long we have been friends, have I ever tried anything? Don't you trust me?'

'It's not that.'

'Then?'

'We should wait till we are married.'

'We are waiting,' he answered. 'What else am I doing?' He took her chin in his hands. 'Life after life we have been together. No one can separate us.'

Still she looked unhappy.

'Look, we have known each other two years. Have I ever taken advantage of you? But in the Univ. lawns people are always looking, it is not so nice, *yaar*. Don't you also feel?' he implored.... Again he tried to push her down and this time she acquiesced. He put her feet in his lap, even her feet made him mad, he said, as he fondled them, dirty and dusty, a sign of how truly he accepted her. He began to caress her all over, and her mind divided one part on college and parents, one part following his hypnotic touch. Then one hand snaked around the buttons of her *kurta* and the muscles under her skin tightened.

'No,' she protested, pushing him away.

'Relax, I am not doing anything,' he whispered near her cheek. Slowly he inserted his hand inside. His eyes closed, and his breathing grew heavier. He gave a small moan. 'I could die for you *yaar*, you are my princess, my queen for the rest of my life there is only you.'

She tried to respond in kind but the words did not come.

Suresh was lulled enough to reach under her *kurta* for the tape that kept her *salwar* up. This time she pushed him away with all her might.

'I'm not staying,' she announced, sitting up.

'Are you angry with me? Have I done something? he pleaded.

'Take me back.'

What is wrong with you? Haven't we known each other a long time? Didn't you trust me enough to come with me here alone?

> He made it sound as though she had committed a crime. She turned away her head.
>
> Here Suresh threw himself on Nisha and began to wail, 'I love you, I love you, why are you so cruel to me?'
>
> 'I love you too,' she cried, tears wetting her face, her hanky, his shoulder, as he pulled her, resisting, to him.
>
> Eventually they left the room. (191-92)

Although disbelief hung in the air yet Nisha stood pass before the time. She had a flair for studies which she carried on till the end of her strife. Initially she wanted to have intercaste marriage for which she was not allowed. Later on she wanted to carry on her study that too was not permitted by the fear of disgrace:

> What had been buried all these years in the recesses of her mind now came back to haunt her. Vicky rubbing against her, Vicky with his hand under her panties, asking her to touch it, grabbing her hand and sticking his thing into it, jerking her hand up and down, Vicky pressing himself into her while she was trying to do her home work. Suresh moaning beside her, at the height of their passion, holding her hand over him, while she, uncertainly trying to please, gripped it tentatively through her underwear as he climaxed.
>
> Thinking of Vicky she thought of Suresh; thinking of Suresh drove her back to Vicky. If, with Suresh's arms around her, she could reveal what had happened all those years ago, she would be absolved. No matter what her cousin had done to her, he, Suresh, had touched her in love; theirs was love, nothing else.
>
> She tried to keep her mind on love and purity, but the past intruded she wanted to run screaming from herself. Was there never to relief from her thoughts? She imagined the acid used to scour toilets, yellow, evil-smelling liquid sold in old beer bottles, the strongest cleaner she knew. If only she could dip a rag in that, run it under her skin, swab her mind with it, dissolve the foul stuff so that it lost the power to affect, now and for ever. (208-09)

Finally, Nisha anchored her own business called business woman of stitching the suits which went till her own children came in this world. She is the best example of the heroine who suffered a lot throughout her life but lastly the novelist seemed to prove that it never rains but it pours. That was why she got married and also blessed with two issues. The main protagonist of the novel—Nisha—the manglik, around whom the whole novel revolves—finally gets rid of the parental home and claustrophobia and takes haven in a new home of her own dreams after getting married with Arvind another manglik of the same caste—a home in which there is no chorus, no tension rather intention and too much care of the mother-in-law for her twins—boy and girl. The novelist shuts the curtain of the novel happily with these words:

> Ten months after Nisha's marriage, twins were born. One girl, one boy. Her duty was over—God had been kind, however hard it was to believe. (336)

Told in a sustained colloquial voice, *Home*[6] is startling in its sweep and unerringly accurate in the bleakness and hope it presents.[7] When Manju Kapur makes a little fish speak, it speaks like a whale.[8] When she discusses a point, she lectures like a stern teacher and stares her readers in the face. It is very rich and intricate novel and each successive reading reveals new significance and new layers of meaning. Its complexities are endless and so equally are the interpretation it has received at the hand of critics.

On the other hand, Kiran Desai's *The Inheritance of Loss*[9] is a rich, expansive work. It's about globalization, immigration and class, and Desai is now among a growing group of prominent young novelists of Indian background, including Arundhati Roy and Jhumpa Lahiri. The novel seeks the study of the lives of hypocrisy through the character of Gyan so called Mathematics tutor. Kiran Desai reveals in one of the interviews, "I think there are several kinds of loss that happen in this book. It is really a book about characters that have been forced to live half-lives or lives of hypocrisy because of the circumstances that they find themselves in. I found that when I writing it, everyone had that half-story to tell, which together added up to a picture that I felt was whole." In the words of Roxana Robinson, "A Whirlwind of a novel, rich and sad and funny. Kiran Desai moves between New York and the northeast corner of India; between the sense of lose and the sense of possession; between the big notion of colonialism and the small notion of intimacy. Desai's enchanting—often hilarious—descriptions are a pleaser to read."[10]

This majestic novel of a busy, grasping time—every moment holding out the possibility of hope or betrayal, set in the mid-1980s in Kalimpong, high in the northeastern Himalayas, centres on three people and one dog living together in an ancient house named Cho Oyu. There's the embittered, reptilian judge, lost in his chessboard and in his memories: of a youth spent at Cambridge many decades earlier; of humiliation in a foreign land. Staying with him (in this order of affection received) are his beloved dog Mutt and his 17-year-old granddaughter Sai, who was orphaned as a child. The judge's cook, who manages the household, and a few neighbours scattered around the area, round off the cast. As the story unfolds, insurgency is growing in the region: the Indian Nepalese want their own country or state, a Gorkhaland where they will not be treated as servants; young boys, trying to be men, roam the mountainside looting houses, collecting ammunition. Their predicament is contrasted against that of Indians settled abroad (the cook's son Biju, stumbling from one job to the next in the US, in a humorous parallel narrative).

Sai,[11] who was studying in St. Augustine's Convent, heard the news of the death of her parents who were crashed by the local bus wheels, made her orphaned and compelled to take haven in the house of retired Judge residing in isolated house at the foot of Mount Kanchenjunga in Himalayas. Judge was served by a faithful cook who was always lost in memory of his lovable son Biju illegally immigrant in New York for job. The Judge first appointed Nonita or Noni as a tutor to teach Sai—Science to Shakespeare. It was only when Noni's abilities in Maths and Science began to falter when Sai was sixteen that the Judge was forced to hire Gyan twenty years old pal to take over these subjects. It was Feb. 1986, Sai was seventeen and her romance with Gyan, the mathematics tutor was not even a year old:

> Could fulfillment ever be felt as deeply as loss? Romantically she decided that love must surely reside in the gap between desire and fulfillment, in the lack, not the contentment. Love was the ache, the anticipation, the retreat, everything around it but the emotion itself. (2-3)

When Gyan came to teach Sai the very first day his eyes rested directly upon her as if he were eating her alive in an orgy of the imagination. That night Sai sat and starred into the mirror:

> Sitting across from Gyan, she had felt so acutely aware of herself, she was certain it was because of his gaze on her, but every time she glanced up, he was looking in another direction. (74)

Over the days, she found herself continually obsessed with her own face, aware that she was meanwhile whiting her aptitude for something else. When Sai became interested in love, she became interested in other people's love affairs, and she pestered the cook about the judge and his wife. The novelist depicted the lives of their hypocrisy step by step in the novel in an exotic manner as if the novelist might have experienced in her life. In the drawing room sitting with newspapers, Sai and Gyan were left alone, quite alone, for the first time. Their eyes read on industriously, but their thoughts did not cleave to such discipline, and finally Gyan, unable to bear this any longer, this tightrope tension between them, put down his paper with a crashing sound, turned abruptly toward her, and blurted:

> "Do you put oil in your hair?"
>
> "No," she said, startled. "I never do."
>
> After a bit of silence, "Why?" she asked. Was there something wrong with her hair?
>
> "I can't hear you—the rain is so loud," he said, moving closer.
>
> "What?"
>
> "Why?"
>
> "It looks so shiny I thought you might."

"No."

"It looks very soft," he observed. "Do you wash it with shampoo?"

"Yes."

"What kind?"

"Sunsilk."

Oh, the unbearable intimacy of brand names, the boldness of the questions.

"What soap?"

"Lux."

"Beauty bar of the film stars?"

"Let me see your hands. They are so small."

"Are they?"

"Yes." He held his own out by hers. "See?"

Fingers' nails.

"*Hm*. What long fingers. Little nails. But look, you bite them."

He weighed her hand.

"Light as a sparrow. The bones must be hollow." (114)

So they played the game of courtship, reading, retreating, teasing, molesting, intoxicating and fleeing. "*Kiss me*!" He pleaded. "No," she said, delighted and terrified. Moments clocked by precisely, and finally she could not bear it—she closed her eyes and felt the terrified measure of his lips on hers, trying to match one shape with the other. And there was a flood of kisses one after another without a moment's delay:

"Nose?" He kissed it.

"Eyes?" Eyes.

"Ears?" Ears.

"Cheek?" Cheek.

"Fingers." one, two, three, four, five.

"The other hand, please." Ten kisses.

"Toes?" (125)

Thus Gyan and Sai's romance was flourishing. The novelist captured the moment in the novel pornographically:

> She picked up the judge's powder puff, unbuttoned her blouse, and powdered her breasts. She hooked up her blouse again and that puff, so foreign, so silken, she stuffed inside; she was too grown-up for childish thieving, she knew, but she was filled with greed [...]. He clamped down on her, tussled her to the floor, and as more of that perfect rose complexion, blasted into a million motes, came filtering down, in a dense frustration of lust and fury—penis uncoiling, mottled purple—black as if with rage, blundering, uncovering the chute he had heard rumor of—he stuffed his way ungracefully into her [...]. Your eyes are lovely, dark and deep [...]. Drink to me only with thine eyes. (166, 169)

The character of Gyan is depicted by the novelist like the butterfly tasting and sipping the pollen from different flowers and resting no where. In one of the scenes Gyan was found by Sai red handed in voluptuous critical situation: "Does Gyan live here?" Sai asked despite herself (256). Suspicion shadowed the girl's face. It was an old, unsurprised sureness of ulterior motives, a funny look in a child. "He's my mathematics tutor." answered the other girl (256). Still looking as if someone like Sai could only mean trouble, she set down the pot and went back into the house as the rooster rushed forth to peck the grain stuck at the bottom, climbing right inside, giving the hens a reprieve. At that moment, Gyan came out, caught her expression of distaste before she had a chance to disguise it, and was outraged. Gyan said, "How dare she seek him out to find her indulgence in pity!" (256). He had been feeling guilty about his extended silence, was considering returning to see her, but now he knew he was quite right. The rooster climbed out of the port and began to strut about. He was the only grand thing around, crowned, spurred, crowing like a colonial: "What do you want?" asked Gyan (257). She saw his thoughts recast his eyes and mouth, remembered that he had abandoned her, not the other way around, and she was bitterly angry:

> Dirty hypocrite.
>
> Pretending one thing, living another. Nothing but lies through and through. (257)

Above everything else, though, *The Inheritance of Loss* is a tender meditation on loving and loss. It is about how, in all our different ways, we wish to fit in. The fact of exile and how that exile affects the notion of home, how it colours perception and how it heightens the sense of wanting to belong are strong currents that run through this novel and make it a parable of times.

In a generous vision, sometimes funny, sometimes sad, Desai presents the human quandaries facing panoply of characters.[12] Whatever be the love and deportment of Gyan to Sai but Sai thought with a burst of hope. A message: I will love you after all and the novel sums up happily:

> The five peaks of Kanchenjunga turned golden with the kind of luminous light that made you feel, if briefly, that truth was apparent. All you needed to do was to reach out and pluck it. (324)

Salman Rushdie, a family friend, describes their divergent styles this way: "Anita is a deceptively quiet writer. Kiran is a little bit more showy as a writer. There is a little more flamboyance in the prose." Unlike her mother, Desai said she doesn't think of marrying or having children. "The isolation of writing settles in too deeply. It becomes part of your personality and your life," she said. "If I had a child, I'd have to break out of it and be sweet. But as a writer I am trying to understand hate and anger." Lately, Desai said, she has been longing for the solitude of writing to pull her back in. She glanced wistfully outside at the rain and the wet landscape, reminiscent this afternoon of Kalimpong.[13] Earlier this month, at the age 35, she became the youngest woman ever to win Britain's Man Booker Prize, for her novel *The Inheritance of Loss*—a career-stirring event for any budding novelist, but particularly so in her case, because it is an honour that has eluded her celebrated mother, Anita Desai, who has been a finalist three times for the prize.

Suffice to say both the novelists treated the sex and romance in their novels—one through the characters of Nisha, Vicky and Suresh as in *Home* and other through the characters of Sai and Gyan as in *The Inheritance of Loss*. In the fitness of the things it can be quoted that very genuine problem of one female being reflected by another female is the outcome of the novels and the novelists give the message to the society that female are not always at the fault as they are treated and rejected, they are used, misused and finally abused. With the changing scenario I do agree with the words of Shakespeare who celebrates the same theme in *Othello* through Emilia, wife of Iago (Act-III, Scene-iii):

> 'Tis not a year or two shows us a man:
>
> They are all but stomachs; we all but food:
>
> They eat us hungrily, and when they are full
>
> They belch us.

NOTES

1. One of the interviews published in the *Hindustan Times* dated 16 April 2006.
2. One of the interviews published in the *Hindustan Times* dated 16 April 2006.
3. The same idea is discernible in the following views of Tennyson who claims:

   Men for the field, women for the hearth,
   Men with the sword, for the needle she,
   Men with the head, women with the heart,
   Men to command, women to obey,
   All else confusion.
4. Herbert also reveals the same idea in the following words:

   Words are women, deeds are men.
5. Quoted by Kiran Nagarkar who revealed about this bard:

   Manju Kapur is one of the most perceptive chroniclers of that microcosm of the nation state: the joint family. The narrative voice is deceptively soft, for Kapur lays it all bare-conflicting loyalties, intrigues, triumphs and tragedies. Manju Kapur. *Home* (New Delhi: Random House India, 2006) Cover page.

6. Manju Kapur. *Home* (New Delhi: Random House India, 2006). All the rest excerpts are quoted from the same book.
7. Quoted by Nilanjana Roy who unveiled:

   'Few writers have explored the complex terrain of the Indian family with as much insight and affection as Manju Kapur. She describes the small rebellions and intense power struggles with a knowledge of the human heart that is at once compelling and terrifying.' Manju Kapur. *Home*, Cover page.
8. In one of her interviews published in the *Sunday Hindustan Times* dated 22 January 2006 Desai herself unlocked, "I have really tried to capture the patterns—the emotional and historical patterns that I have witnessed. It has been a history that is caught between East and West and traveling back and forth."
9. Kiran Desai. *The Inheritance of Loss* (New Delhi: Penguin Books India Ltd., January 2006). All the rest excerpts are quoted from the same book.
10. Quoted by Roxana Robinson. Kiran Desai. *The Inheritance of Loss* (New Delhi: Penguin Books India Ltd., January 2006) Cover page.
11. Like Sai, the teenager in the novel, Desai attended a convent school in Kalimpong, where her family also had a summer home. In the novel, Sai falls in love with the impoverished Gyan, whose Nepalese family once provided cheap labor for tea plantations. The novel takes place in the 1980s, when ethnic Nepalese rebelled. "They didn't have political and economic power", she said. "It suddenly skidded into violence." The Nepalese immigrant story, she said, parallels that of Biju in America, and of immigrant groups everywhere.
12. Quoted by Binnie Kirshenbaum, Kiran Desai. *The Inheritance of Loss*. Cover page. He further unearths: "A nation's tragedies, great and small are revealed through the hopes and the dreams, the innocence and the assonance, the love betrayed and the all—too human failings of a superbly realized cast of characters".
13. *Inheritance*, her second novel, was much harder to write than *Hullabaloo*, she said, taking "seven years of my being determinedly isolated". It almost didn't get published in England. "The British said it didn't work", Desai said. Nearly 10 houses rejected it until Hamish Hamilton bought it.

2

Accomplished versus Jeopardized Literary Excellence: A Comparative Study of Amitav Ghosh's *The Hungry Tide* and Kiran Desai's *The Inheritance of Loss*

Nilanshu Kumar Agarwal

D.C. Chambial, one of the significant contemporary poets from Himachal Pradesh, and the winner of the prestigious Michael Madhusudan Academy Award for his poetry, told me in an interview the significance of symbols and curved language in poetry: "These symbols...make the reader sit up and think about the exact thing that the poet wants to suggest by using such symbols.... I think, symbols give more delight and the bliss...and play a vital role in fulfilling one major objective of giving pleasure. I personally do not relish a direct or flat poetry." The beauty of creative literature lies in its suggestiveness. It may open several meanings, when a *Sahridaya* Reader (connoisseur of art and literature) goes through it. Beneath the text, several layers of sub-text lie hidden. Imaginative literature or poetry has at least two meanings—manifest meaning and latent meaning. Manifest or literal meaning is the meaning at the primary or external level of understanding. If we use the terminology of Chomsky, this literal, primary, manifest or external meaning refers to 'competence'. Here, it must be stated that Chomsky had made a linguistic distinction between 'competence' and 'performance'. While 'competence' is the standard version of the language, 'performance' refers to the deviation from the standard conventions and norms of language. A creative artist of literature is concerned with this deviation from the orthodox meaning of a word. This deviation or metaphorical twist to language is the very basis of all symbolism or indirect communication in literature. When Eliot began *The Waste Land* by pointing out 'April is the cruellest month', he was indicating at the sterility of the modern man. On the surface Eliot appears to be talking about April, but in reality it is the signifier of the contemporary degraded and apathetic society. This month has become 'the cruellest month' for us, which is generally considered a month of fertility, vegetation, fun and ecstasy. In a way, through this symbol of April, Eliot signifies that the values have gone haywire in the modern Europe, filled with eerie ennui.

Thus, literature does consist of two types of meanings—literal and figurative. This distinction between two kinds of meanings has parallels in Saussure's classification of 'langue' and 'parole'. 'Langue' is the ordinary and everyday use of language, while 'parole' is the creative deviation from the traditional language. R.S. Sharma in his discussion about I.A. Richards' book *The Philosophy of Rhetoric* explains tenor as "the general drift" (62).

This general drift in the meaning of a particular expression opens several layers of aesthetic pleasure for the reader. Literature, to be very honest, is pseudo or curved statement. That is, literature hides within itself more than it reveals to the naked eye. Only the microscopic eye of a *Sahridaya* Reader can unearth the latent meaning. R.S. Pathak, in his book *Vakrokti and Stylistics Concepts*, explains this poetic/literary deviation or innovation thus, "...the language of poetry allows him licences for making unprecedented innovations by exploiting grammatical possibilities of the language" (73). Kunjunni Raja, while discussing Anandavardhana's *Dhvanyaloka*, holds almost the similar view:

> In the *Dhvanyaloka*, Anandavardhana establishes his theory that suggestion is the soul of poetry. He says that

> beautiful ideas in poetry are of two kinds: literal and implied. The latter is something like charm in girls which is distinct from the beauty of the various parts of the body; this implied sense is something more than the literal meaning.... This suggested sense is not understood by those who merely know grammar and lexicon; it is understood only by men of taste who know the essence of poetry. This suggested sense is the most important element in poetry; in fact it is the soul of poetry. (287-88)

Thus, every great literary piece has several layers of meanings. In the present paper, I propose to discuss Amitav Ghosh's *The Hungry Tide* as a great piece of literature and also to contrast its reputation with another very popular novel, Kiran Desai's *The Inheritance of Loss*. The objective of this paper is to contrast the literary merits of these two novels.

The title of the titanic work of imagination from the pen of Ghosh is highly symbolic. Like all imaginative literature the title of *The Hungry Tide*, called "a curious mixture of scientific treatise, travelogue and folklore" by Partha Chatterjee, also has a suggestive meaning. G.B. Mohan has analysed this concept of implied/suggestive meaning in poetry (imaginative literature) thus:

> Beauty in poetry consists in the predominance of the suggested tertiary meaning over the primary referential and the secondary contextual meanings...the essence of poetry is not what is directly expressed but what is indirectly suggested. All poets find out directions by indirections. They resort to metaphor, paradox, hyperbole and other figures of speech because the direct and straight way of expression is not adequate to objectify their experience. (19)

What G.B. Mohan has commented about poetry is applicable to all imaginative literature in general and *The Hungry Tide* in particular. In a way, the title of this novel has several layers of meaning. On the external, primary or manifest level, it is indicative of voracious and carnivorous tidal region of the Sundarbans. This novel deals with "the archipelago called the

Sundarbans off the easternmost coast of India, between the sea and plains of Bengal" (Hawley, 14).

The treatment of natural and geographical surroundings in the novel is quite unlike Wordsworth's adoration of the same. The great romantic poet worshipped nature for its 'beauteous forms'. His idealization of nature was marked by imaginative romantic illusions. He just saw the rosy side of the nature, which is far removed from reality. There is other side of the coin too. Sometimes nature may be as disastrous, chaotic and havoc-friendly as Gorgon's head. Nature is not just the representative of 'the stars of midnight' and 'the floating clouds'. The other side of the nature is very heinous. Will the Tsunami victims be able to sing of nature in 'full-throated ease'? How can the millions of people living in the regions of Greater Himalayas find Wordsworth's idealization of nature comfortable, when there are continuous threats to their lives from the killers like earthquakes and landslides? Every year, there are natural disasters of famine, drought and flood, claiming numberless lives. So, in my view Wordsworth's glorification of nature is illusory and he closed his eyes to the cruel aspects of nature. He did not see that some times, nature may become a rough beast, hungry of human blood. If we compare Wordsworth with one of Shavian characters, it is Raina of *Arms And The Man*, who comes quite close to Wordsworth's imaginative idealization of nature. Raina in the just-mentioned play [which is called "an amusing satire on military heroes" (609) by W.J. Long] has illusory notions about love and war. She idealizes both of them; similarly Wordsworth adores the mother nature without the slight whiff of realism. Later on, coming in contact with Bluntschli, the chocolate-cream soldier, she realizes her mistake. A genuine reader of good literature experiences the inadequacy of Wordsworth's treatment of nature, when he encounters the life-threatening dangers, posed by nature in real life.

At this juncture, it will be proper to say that a better, fuller and a more realistic approach is adopted by Amitav Ghosh in *The Hungry Tide*, which was called "a compelling book" by W.R. Greer. The mingling of realism and imagination in the presentation of nature exhibits Ghosh's extreme devotion to his art. His picture of nature appears to be complete and it does not smack of any false sentimentalism or illusory romanticization of the subject.

In his realistic handling of the subject, Ghosh presents nature as hungry of human blood. Hungry tide stands for all the disastrous aspects of nature. For this unfriendly approach of nature, we may mark the following expression about mangrove forest from the script, which was being read by Kanai in the novel:

> A mangrove forest is a universe unto itself,... Mangrove leaves are tough and leathery, the branches gnarled and the foliage often impassably dense. Visibility is short and the air still and fetid. At no moment can human beings have any doubt of the terrain's utter hostility to their presence, of its cunning and resourcefulness, of its determination to destroy or expel them. Every year dozens of people perish in the embrace of that dense foliage, killed by tigers, snakes and crocodiles. (7-8)

The aforesaid extract from the novel shows the extremely hostile approach of the nature towards the man. In the section "Canning", Kanai froze in disbelief on seeing the plight of the passengers in the boat due to 'the vast expanse of the billowing mud':

> On stepping off the plank, there was a long-drawn out moment when each passenger sank slowly into the mud, like a spoon disappearing into a very thick *daal*; only when they were in up to their hips did their descent end and their forward movement begin. With their legs hidden from sight, all that was visible of their struggles was the twisting of their upper bodies. (24-25)

In the section entitled "S. Daniel", Nirmal and Kanai are discussing S. Daniel's efforts in bringing people to the tidal region, which was fraught with numberless risks to their lives. The furious picture of the tidal surroundings is highly pathetic:

> Think of what it was like: think of the tigers, crocodiles and snakes that lived in the creeks and *nalas* that

> covered the islands. This was a feast for them. They killed hundreds of people. (52)

In the same vein, when Piya falls in the sea, 'the muddy brown water was rushing up to meet her face'. This incident of Piya's fall provokes in the reader's heart the *Bibhatsa* rasa or the rasa of indignation. Here, it must be stated that rasa for the reader is the aesthetic experience in literature. A genuine reader experiences this aesthetic feeling, when he reads a truly imaginative piece of literature. There are certain *Sthayibhavas* or permanent emotions of the reader, which lie dormant in his heart. When the reader encounters a genuinely imaginative literature, that creative work awakens the lasting/permanent emotion and the result is the origin of rasa or aesthetic experience. About this process of aesthetic experience, G.B. Mohan writes thus:

> Every human being is born with a set of instinctual propensities inherited from earlier generations, and deposited on the bed of his consciousness.... They are called *sthayi* (permanent), because they always remain embedded in human organism. It is generally agreed that there are nine such emotions possessed by all human beings.... In poetic experience the latent emotional traces are aroused. (14-15)

In the sudden fall of this cetologist, our latent emotion of disgust is aroused, when she is covered with dirty mud. This cetologist on a mission "to study the habits and habitats of the Gangetic dolphins" (Ray, 41) falls in the muddy tidal water and this picture of ugly nature arouses our latent emotion of disgust (*jugupsa*) and the result is the release of *Bibhatsa* rasa (rasa of indignation):

> With her breath running out, she felt herself to be enveloped inside a cocoon of eerie glowing murk and could not tell whether she was looking up or down. In her head there was a smell, or rather, a metallic savour she knew to be, not blood, but inhaled mud. It had entered her mouth, her nose, her throat, her eyes—it had become a shroud closing in on her, folding her in its cloudy wrappings. She threw her hands at it, scratching,

> lunging, pummeling, but its edges seemed always to recede, like the slippery walls of a placental sac. Then she felt something brush against her back and at that moment there was no touch that would not have made her respond as if to the probing of a reptilian snout. (54-55)

The picture of the all encompassing mud in the expressions like 'a shroud closing in on her' and 'folding her in its cloudy wrappings' along with its comparison with 'the slippery walls of a placental sac' can definitely evoke the feelings of disgust and repugnance in the reader's heart. The plight of Piya is sure to create in the readers a weird feeling of distaste for nature. Nature is seen in its worst form here.

At the outset of the paper I had mentioned that every good piece of literature has manifest and latent meanings. While the literal meaning of *The Hungry Tide* refers to the fury of wild nature in the tidal country, the metaphorical or symbolic connotation of the same carries a lot of psychological and philosophical weight. Metaphorically, the title of the novel refers to the emotional tide, in which the characters of the novel are caught and which is devouring whole of their personality. The experiences and relations of the characters with other persons are highly tempestuous and tumultuous, reminding the readers of the furious sea-waves of the tidal country.

If we judge some of the major characters of the novel, we find the tempest/tide of psychological and social problems pervading them from top to bottom. Take for instance the character of Piyali Roy, whose parents are of Bengali origin and who is not well-versed in Bengali language, as she was born and brought up in Seattle, U.S.A. She is in the tidal country to make a study of the dolphins. During her stay in India, she experiences a sort of alienation/mental torture because of her exotic appearance. The one important problem, which she encounters, is the problem of communication. At the railway station, she was enquiring about the train to Canning. Her plight is described thus:

> One of the onlookers began to explain, gesticulating with an upraised arm. But the explanation was in Bengali and it was lost on her. She stopped the man with a raised hand and said, in apology, that she knew no Bengali. (4)

Then, the approach of the guide and the guard on the ship was clearly marked by animosity for a person of another culture. Here, Ghosh is indicating that in contemporary society, people are suffering from jingoistic and ethnocentric prejudices, which are creating hurdles in the promotion of a multi-lingual, multi-ethnic and multi-cultural world ethos. Due to certain cultural and racial prejudices, there is very little interaction or dialogue among the citizens of the world.

The actions of Mej-da (the guide) towards Piya are obviously objectionable. The situation is described thus by Ghosh:

> Then, to her surprise, Mej-da ordered all the helpers to leave the launch. Evidently the crew was to consist of no one other than himself and the guard. Why just these two and no one else? There was something about this that was not quite right. She watched in concern as the boys filed off the launch and her misgivings only deepened when Mej-da proceeded to enact a curious little pantomime, as if to welcome her on his vessel.... But the performance ended with a gesture both puzzling and peculiarly obscene. Bursting into laughter, he gesticulated in the direction of his tongue and his crotch. She looked away quickly, frowning, puzzled as to the meaning of this bizarre coda. (33-34)

This clash of the civilizations and cultures, which Piyali Roy experiences, is also seen in the plight of the settlers at Morichjhapi. In the depiction of the precarious situation, faced by Piyali Roy and the settlers at Morichjhapi, Ghosh is speaking against the narrowness of the human heart. The world is 'a melting pot' or 'a salad bowl' on account of the simultaneous presence of numberless communities and groups, belonging to different religions, castes and nationalities. But the contemporary man, with his apathetic approach towards 'the significant other', has made the world a sterile wasteland. The Britain based Guyanese author David Dabydeen uses the image of a 'beehive' to describe the cultural diversity of a city like London. G. Rai has elaborated this concept of Dabydeen thus:

> A number of different cultural groups are present in one place with little communication between them taking place. Each is confined to its own cell. Britons do not spend long enough in the West Indian cells nor do they invite West Indians to their cells either. (16)

This alienation/depression of 'the significant other' in the novel on account of the narrow cultural prejudices of the people clearly indicates that the hungry tide of cultural clash is excessively harmful and disturbing for the world.

Another major issue, significantly touched by Ghosh in the novel, is the man-woman relationship. There are several shades of the relationship between the two sexes in the novel. Almost all the major characters of the novel are submerged by the tidal waves of this relationship. Take for example, Kanai, who "liked to think that he had the true connoisseur's ability to both praise and appraise women" (Ghosh, 3). On account of this illusory notion about himself, he makes attempts to establish relationship with Piya; but fails. He appears to be a notorious womanizer. His comment about Moyna—"I'd say Moyna is the kind of woman who would be good for a brief but exciting dalliance" (220)—rectifies the just-mentioned assumption. The women sense it, hence his love exploits end in failure. He is envious of Fokir, who is able to establish emotional contact with Piya despite the communication barrier between the two. Kanai, about whom the novelist had said—"Language was both his livelihood and his addiction" (4), is unable to communicate with the heart of Piya, while the illiterate fisherman is able to enter the emotional tide of her heart. The complex of Piya's emotional attachment for Fokir and the simultaneous envy of Kanai for the fisherman is conspicuous in the following conversation between Piya and Kanai:

> ...Very few people can adapt themselves to that kind of rhythm—one in a million, I'd say. That is why it was so amazing to come across someone like Fokir.
>
> Amazing? Why?
>
> 'You saw how he spotted that dolphin there, didn't you?', said Piya. 'It's like he's always watching the water—even without being aware of it. I have worked with many experienced fishermen before but I've never met anyone with such an incredible instinct: it's as if he can see right into the river's heart.' (267)

When Piya admires Fokir, the tidal onslaught of envy raids Kanai. While the turbulent waves of jealousy are dashing against the shores of Kanai's heart, the tranquil waves of soft love for Fokir are touching the innermost chords of Piya's heart. Mark the following dialogue between Kanai and Piya again:

> Is there anyone else you could work with?
>
> 'It wouldn't be the same, Kanai,' Piya said. 'Fokir's abilities as an observer are really extraordinary. I wish I could tell you what it was like to be with him these last few days—it was one of the most exciting experiences of my life.'
>
> A sudden stab of envy provoked Kanai to make a mocking aside. 'And all that while, you couldn't understand a word he was saying, could you?'
>
> 'No,' she said, with a nod of acknowledgment. 'But you know what? There was so much in common between us it didn't matter.'
>
> 'Listen,' said Kanai, in a flat, harsh voice. 'You shouldn't deceive yourself, Piya: there wasn't anything common between you then and there isn't now. Nothing. He's a fisherman and you're a scientist....' (268)

Here, it must be stated that there is in Fokir this instinctive warmth and child like naive simplicity, which bind him spontaneously to the women. That is why, Piya falls in love with him. Moyna, his wife, grows anxious, when she finds the proximity of Piya towards Fokir. Moyna knows well that

Fokir's spontaneous innocence is sure to create emotional ripples in Piya. The concern of Moyna due to the relationship between Piya and Fokir is clearly visible in her following conversation with Kanai:

> '...And I'm glad you're going, Kanai-babu.'
>
> 'Why?' said Kanai. 'Are you tired of bringing me my meals?'
>
> 'No,' she said. 'It's not that.'
>
> 'Then?'
>
> 'I'm just glad that you'll be there, Kanai-babu; that they won't be alone.'
>
> 'Who?'
>
> 'The two of them.' Her voice was suddenly serious.
>
> 'You mean Fokir and Piya?' (257)

Besides these issues pertaining to man-woman relationship, the novel deals with several other themes, related to human society. A number of tangling problems of contemporary social order are surveyed in the novel. In a way, the title of the novel is suggestive of plethora of human and social issues; the hungry tide is nothing but the hungry human tide. It throws light on the tidal waves of universal emotions, present in every human heart.

Thus, the title of the novel is highly suggestive and symbolic. It has at least two layers of meaning—manifest and latent. The excellence of Ghosh, "a champion of post-modern cultural weightlessness" (John Mee, 325), lies in the fact that beneath the explicitly revealed primary meaning, there is sufficient hidden or metaphorical meaning in the title of the novel. That is why, the novel has been extensively admired by the scholars. For instance, Amardeep Singh calls it "the work of a novelist at the peak of his powers". R.K. Dhawan too remarks about the novel, "Epical in scope, the novel has captured readers' imagination the world over" (10).

I will now shift my attention to Kiran Desai's *The Inheritance of Loss*, about which Pankaj Mishra comments thus, "Although it focuses on the fate of a few powerless individuals, Kiran Desai's extraordinary new novel manages to explore, with intimacy and insight, just about every contemporary international issue: globalization, multi-culturalism, economic inequality, fundamentalism and terrorist violence. Despite being set in the mid-1980's, it seems the best kind of post-9/11 novel." The remaining part of this paper will analyse whether Desai's novel has those pearls of literary imagination, which are scattered all around in Ghosh's work.

Kiran Desai's Man Booker award winning novel, *The Inheritance of Loss* discusses several tangling international social and cultural issues, giving rise to a seething feeling of despair in the hearts of the readers. The first bewildering problem, raised by Desai is that of the immigrant and diasporic sensibility. The disturbed mental condition of the displaced immigrants has caught the imagination of several Postcolonial novelists and Desai is no exception. Stephen Gill, India-born Canadian poet and novelist, has remarked thus about the diasporic sensibility:

> Diaspora essentially is a bitter experience of dislocation that leads to alienation, a sense of loss and nostalgic desires. It refers to that particular class of immigrants who are unable to go back.... Usually, Diasporans are not happy anywhere, and suffer silently.... (*Bridge-in-Making*, 54)

This sense of alienation among the immigrants caught the attention of Desai and she created the diasporic characters like Biju and Saeed, who, to borrow an expression of Stephen Gill, have the psychologically disturbing elements of "alienation, loss...memories of the past and dream to return to the land of birth" (*Discovering Stephen Gill*, 123-24). These characters experience displacement and nostalgia in the alien land. In a way, the memory of the imaginary homelands always haunts the diaspora. Pramod K. Nayar has explained this theme of diasporic sensibility in the following manner:

> Exile and displacement narratives frequently combine a sense of disquiet with their nostalgia and longing. Atwood recreates the world of Susanna Moodi, who migrated from Scotland to Canada in the 1830s, as a

> world in which the migrant is homeless and foreign. Such a migrant does not see the 'new world' as a land of opportunity.... Here Moodie finds herself 'foreign', while others see the new world as a site of freedom. The sense of homelessness is accentuated by the recognition that one has not found a new home in the adopted country. Much of diasporic writing explores the theme of an original home. This original home as now lost—due to their exile—is constantly worked into the imagination and myth of the displaced individual/community. Nostalgia is therefore a key theme in diasporic writing. (191)

Similarly Salman Rushdie, too in his celebrated critical book *Imaginary Homelands*, emphasizes the importance of nostalgia for an author. In the introductory essay of the book, Rushdie has mentioned the dilemma of the authors in settling in alien countries. A feeling of guilt engulfs most of the immigrant authors, as they had left their homelands and the orthodox ideologies. They "straddle two cultures". However, this distance from the homeland is the source of tremendous fertility in an author. This longing for the homelands in alien lands is the genesis of artistic creativity for the authors. Salman Rushdie is one of the chief initiators of these nostalgic moods in his fiction and his critical book *Imaginary Homelands* is no exception. It is this obsessive affection for the past homeland that encourages him to have the portrait of his ancestral house in his present room. *Imaginary Homelands* begins with the artistic description of the just-mentioned portrait: "An old photograph in a cheap frame hangs on a wall of the room where I work. It's a picture dating from 1946 of a house into which, at the time of its taking, I had not yet been born. The house is rather peculiar—a three-storeyed gabled affair with tiled roofs and round towers in two corners, each wearing a pointy tiled hat" (9). The same nostalgia motivates Rushdie to visit the house:

> ...I went to visit the house in the photograph and stood outside it, neither daring nor wishing to announce myself to its owners. (I didn't want to see how they'd

> ruined the interior.) I was overwhelmed. The photograph had naturally been taken in black and white; and my memory, feeding on such images as this, had begun to see my childhood in the same way, monochromatically. The colours of my history had seeped out of my mind's eye; now my other eyes were assaulted by colours, by the vividness of the red tiles, the yellow-edged green of cactus-leaves, the brilliance of bougainvillea creeper. (9)

Just like Rushdie, Desai also presents the several psychological shades of Biju, the son of the Judge's cook, who is "hopscothing from one gritty New York restaurant to another on an elusive search for a green card" (backcover of *The Inheritance of Loss*). The predicament of the boy experiencing nostalgia and cultural dislocation in the Western society is well described in these words: "The spirit of these men he worked with amazed Biju, terrified him, overjoyed him, then terrified him again" (15). After the day's work, his fellow workers visited the Dominican women in Washington Heights. But his distaste for these black women is evident, when he eloquently cries out, "How can you? Those, those women are dirty." He calls them "stinking bitches, sounding awkward" (16). His disgust for them is complete, when he utters: "Fucking bitches, fucking cheap women, you'll get some disease; ...smell bad...hubshi...all black and ugly...they make me sick..." (16).

While Biju finds it abnormal due to his orthodox Indian ethos (extra marital sex, being a taboo here in India), his colleague Ronny is quite candid and frank in his confession, "I could do it with a Dog". The episode clearly indicates the cultural contrast—a contrast between the hesitant East and the over-indulgent West. This mocking of one's ideals and believes makes one a prey to feverish anxiety and deadening discomforts. Biju's problems are multiplied by his illegal immigrant status in the States.

Here, it will not be out of place to say that in the just-mentioned episode, Desai has made free use of sex terminology. This episode is not the only one in the novel, where the novelist has given free play of the forbidden fruit.

Sometimes, the language borders on the pulp or cheap pornographic fiction. For example, mark the following titillating expression, where the cook saw a girl in the market:

> She was a lonely girl, small and plump, a glimpse through nightie placket of breasts so buttery that even women who saw them were captivated. (86)

Similarly, the love scene between Gyan and Sai is highly provocative:

> Gyan and Sai. At subsequent pauses in the rain they measured ears, shoulders, and the span of their rib cages.
>
> Collar bones, eyelashes, and chins.
>
> Knees, heels, arch of the feet.
>
> Flexibility of fingers and toes....

Just a week or two later, they were shameless as beggars, pleading for more.

> "Nose?" He kissed it.
>
> "Eyes?" Eyes.
>
> "Ears?" Ears.
>
> "Cheek?" Cheek.
>
> "Fingers." One, two, three, four, five.
>
> "The other hand, please." Ten kisses. (124-25)

What purpose is being served by literature of this type? It is merely to titillate the baser instincts of the humankind. In the wake of Nithari[1] killings of the innocent children by the pedophiles, we must come forward to attack a literature which excites the sex instincts of the people. If the forbidden impulses are aroused by literature and to gratify (let us hope it does not happen in the future) the profane desires, men turn pedophiles, as was reportedly done in Nithari, what is the utility of literature? Is it not merely becoming a plaything in the hands of the nasty people? Here, the supporters of 'art for art's sake' theory may argue that literature should have no social/moral purpose. In the aftermath of the terrorist attack on WTC and most recently the seizure of Mumbai by the gunmen, no literature can be purely aesthetic. It has to be propagandist. To borrow an expression from Rushdie, we should make "as big a fuss, as noisy a complaint about the world as is humanly possible" (99). Rushdie adds: "...there is a genuine need for political fiction, for books that draw new and better maps of reality, and make new languages with which we can understand the world" (100). Thus, literature should focus on some social message. What reform is being done by Desai through this employment of a highly objectionable language—is beyond comprehension. We may also mark the following expression, where the judge Jemubhai is defecating:

> Mid morning he rose from his books, went to the lavatory for the daily trial of his digestion, where he sat straining upon the pot with pained and prolonged effort. As he hear others shuffling outside, waiting for their turn, he stuck a finger up the hole and excavated within, allowing a backed up load of scropulated goat pellets to rattle down loudly.... His finger emerged covered in excrement and blood.... (110-11)

By writing about such type of activity related to defecation, Desai goes beyond the normal in her narrative technique. Particularly, the expressions—'he sat straining upon the pot with pained and prolonged effort', 'he stuck a finger up the hole and excavated within' and 'His finger emerged covered in excrement and blood'—are indigestive and unpalatable.

For whom has the novelist produced such stuff? Who may be prospective readers of this type of fiction? What is the readership of her novel? Naturally, millions of Indians cannot be its readers, because of the ignorance of the natives about the intricacies of English language. Common Indians cannot even comprehend the English newspapers and magazines, what to say of the masterpieces of the Indo Anglians. The supporters of Desai novel may argue that her audience is outside India. Even here, there is a problem. The novel is imbued with Indian words and expressions. How will an outsider understand all this? For example, mark the following expression:

> In Stone Town they ate *samosas* and *chapatis*, *jalebis*, pilau rice.... Saeed and Saeed could sing like Amitabh

> Bachchan and Hema Malini. He sang, "*Mera joota hai japani...*" and "*Bombay se aaya mera dost*—oi!" (53)

The novel is stuffed with these Indian phrases and names. How will a foreigner follow the references to samosas, chapatis, jalebis, Amitabh Bachchan and Hema Malini and the songs from Bollywood?

So, for whom is this work produced? Of course, it is not for the masses. It is in the main written for the public school bred and English speaking pseudo-intellectuals of India. This novel caters just to the tastes and moods of the drawing room idlers. For these snobs, literature is not an emotional experience, rather a tool of social prestige. The classics of the great masters are not works of high imagination for them; they just consider that the mention of a particular work of literature in their conversation will make them smarter. A literary text is no better than a detective piece, as they are not *Sahridaya* Readers (connoisseurs of art and literature). At the outset of this paper, I had mentioned that literature has two types of meanings—literal and figurative. Only the microscopic eye of a *Sahridaya* Reader can unearth the latent meaning.

Thus, a genuine reader is able to derive pleasure out of literature by exploring the inner meaning of a work of literature, while the ordinary and uninspired people just go through the primary meaning. The people of the elite class just take literature at the primary level of understanding, as they discuss literature to exhibit their awareness of the culture and civilization. At this juncture, I am reminded of T.S. Eliot's expression in 'The Love Song of J. Alfred Prufrock':

> In the room the women come and go
>
> Talking of Michelangelo. (3)

What I mean to say is that this novel is just for the elite classes and not for the masses.

Leaving aside this issue of the readership of the novel, I come back to theme of diasporic sensibility in the novel. It is not only Biju, who experiences the racial prejudice; Judge is also the victim of this hydra-headed animosity of the West towards the East. Mark the predicament of the Judge in the following expression:

> Thus Jemubhai's mind had begun to warp; he grew stranger to himself than he was to those around him, found his skin odd-coloured, his own accent peculiar. He forgot how to laugh, could barely manage to lift his lips in a smile, and if he ever did, he held his hand over his mouth, because he could barely let anyone see his gums, his teeth. They seemed too private.... He began to wash obsessively, concerned he would be accused of smelling, and each morning he scrubbed off the thick milky scent of sleep, the barnyard smell that wreathed him when he woke and impregnated the fabric of his pajamas. To the end of his life, he would never be seen without socks and shoes and would prefer shadow to light, faded days to sunny, for he was suspicious that sunlight might reveal him, in his hideousness, all too clearly. (40)

Earlier in the paper, I had mentioned that the novel traces the element of tragic agony in the universe. Another cause of despair in the novel is the non-fulfillment of the demands of the Gorkha Liberation Movement. One of the agitators cries out the woes of the Gorkhas thus:

> At that time, in April of 1947, the Communist Party of India demanded a Gorkhasthan, but the request was ignored.... We are laborers on the tea plantations, coolies dragging heavy loads, soldiers. And are we allowed to become doctors and government workers, owners of the tea plantations? No! We are kept at the level of servants. We fought on behalf of the British for two hundred years. We fought in World War One. We went to East Africa, to Egypt, to the Persian Gulf. We were moved from here to there as it suited them.... We are soldiers, loyal, brave. India or England, they never had cause to doubt our loyalty. In the wars with Pakistan we fought our former comrades on the other side of the border. How our spirit cried. But we are Gorkhas. We are soldiers. Our character has never been

> in doubt. And have we been rewarded?? Have we been given compensation?? Are we given respect?? (158)

Similarly, the love between Gyan and Sai is also not without the ill-effects of the time. Chaotic surrounding situations have robbed the true lovers of the emotional bond and the love between the two is dwindling. Mark the below-mentioned conversation between the two lovers:

> "Well, if you're so clever," she said, "how come you can't even find a proper job? Fail, fail, fail. Every single interview."
>
> "Because of people like you!"
>
> "Oh, because of me...and you're telling me that I am stupid? Who is stupid? Go put it before a judge and we'll see who says is the stupid one." (164)

Thus the novel traces the history of despair and agony in human lives; in a way all the characters of the novel have inherited a sense of loss. Now, the question is—whether the grief painted by Desai in the novel is real or synthetic. Does the novel not present an outsider's response to the problems of the suffering humanity? Kiran Desai, the daughter of Anita Desai, spent the early years of her life in Pune and Mumbai. When she was around nine years old, her family shifted to Delhi. By the time, she turned fourteen, the family moved to England. A year later, they shifted to the United States. Kiran completed her schooling in Massachusetts. She did her graduation from Columbia University.[2] Is a member of the higher strata of life suitable enough to write about the experiences, which he or she has never experienced? Being a member of upper class society, it is very difficult for her to experience the pains of the underdogs of the society. Her response to the predicament of the poor Indians in the West will be considered out of place, as she has not possibly felt the same pain, which Biju in her novel feels. Only a person, who has gone through the pain, can describe the intensity of that injury, as human experience is opaque. Most of the Dalit writers hold the same opinion. They believe that the upper class people, even if they have emotional bond with the Dalits, cannot delineate the age old scar of caste-oppression, as they have not felt it. The notable Dalit writer J.P. Kardam told me in an interview:

> I would like to quote here the words of Dr. Manager Pandey, a renowned Hindi critic, who wrote in the preface to a collection of Dalit short stories edited by Ramnika Gupta that "Only ash knows the experience of burning". This indicates that Dalits know the experience of burning—burning in the fire of sorrows, hatred, disrespect, injustice, inequality and untouchablity. Non-Dalits do not have this experience. Dalits have specific experiences of life, which non-dalits do not have. Only Dalit writers can express their experiences in an authentic manner but not others. Non-Dalit writers may be sympathetic to the Dalits, they may be their well-wishers but their experiences about Dalits are not their self-experiences. They are the observers of torture and exploitation of Dalits, they are not sufferers. (6-7)

To be very honest, the feelings of Kiran Desai for the bottom dogs of the society are synthetic. They are not from the core within, as she was born with a silver spoon in her mouth. She has not experienced the pain, anxiety and grief, which an ordinary human-being encounters. Though the novel has won Man-Booker prize, it is not without defects. Despite several accolades, won by Desai for the novel, it is slightly marred by its synthetic treatment of the subject. In this way, Desai's novel is different from Ghosh's artistic accomplishment in *The Hungry Tide*. While Ghosh achieves superb literary effects in his work, Desai disappoints the readers with her synthetic approach towards the major issues involved.

NOTES

1. Nithari is a place in India, where a number of innocent children were killed by certain heartless killers. The information about this incident may be seen by clicking the following link: <http://www.nitharifacts.com>.
2. The biographical information about Desai is taken from the following source: <http://www.iloveindia.com/indian-heroes/kiran-desai.html>.

WORKS CITED

Agarwal, N.K. "Stephen Gill on His Writing and Diaspora: An Interview." *Discovering Stephen Gill: A Collection of Papers and Articles*. Delhi: Authorspress, 2008.

———. "Only ash knows the experience of burning: An Interview with Dalit Writer Jai Prakash Kardam." *The Quest*, 23.1 (June 2009): 1-8.

———. "D.C. Chambial: In Discussion with Nilanshu Agarwal." *Muse India*, 21 (Sep.-Oct. 2008), July 13, 2009. <http://www.museindia.com/showcurrent10.asp?id=1059>.

Chatterjee, Partha. "Inadequacy of Craft." Rev. of *The Hungry Tide*, by Amitav Ghosh. *Hindu*. July 4, 2004. July 14, 2009. <http://www.hindu.com/lr/2004/07/04/stories/2004070400300100.htm>.

Desai, Kiran. *The Inheritance of Loss*. Penguin, 2006.

Dhawan, R.K. Editorial. *Indian Journal of English Studies*, 42 (2004-2005): 7-10.

Eliot, T.S. *Selected Poems*. Ed. Manju Jain. New Delhi: OUP, 1992.

Ghosh, Amitav. *The Hungry Tide*. 2004. New Delhi: Harper Collins, 2005.

Gill, Stephen. "Mythical Interpretation of Indo-Canadian Diaspora." *Bridge-in-Making*, 50 (Summer 2008): 54-58.

Greer, W.R. "The Tide of Emotion." Rev. of *The Hungry Tide*, by Amitav Ghosh. ReviewsofBooks.com. 2004. July 14, 2009. <http://www.reviewsofbooks.com/hungry_tide/review/>.

Hawley, John C. "Amitav Ghosh's *The Hungry Tide* and the Blurring of National Boundaries." Conference issue of *South Asian Review*, 25.3 (2004): 13-14.

Long, W.J. *English Literature: Its History and its Significance for the Life of the English Speaking World*. Enlarged Edition. Delhi: A.I.T.B.S., 2004.

Mishra, Pankaj. "Wounded by the West." Rev. of *The Inheritance of Loss*, by Kiran Desai. *The New York Times*. Feb. 12, 2006. July 14, 2009. <http://www.nytimes.com/2006/02/12/books/review/12mishra.html>.

Mohan, G.B. *The Response To Poetry: A Study in Comparative Aesthetics*. New Delhi: People's Publishing House, 1968.

Nayar, Pramod K. *Postcolonial Literature: An Introduction.* New Delhi: Pearson Longman, 2008.

Pathak, R.S. *Vakrokti And Stylistic Concept.* New Delhi: Bahri, 1988.

Rai, G. "Postcolonialism: Its Meaning and Significance." *Spiel Journal of English Studies*, 1.2 (2005): 1-22.

Raja, Kunjunni. "Theory of Dhvani." *Indian Aesthetics: An Introduction.* Ed. V.S. Seturaman. Chennai: Macmillan India, 1992, 287-309.

Ray, Rituparna Datta. "*The Hungry Tide*: Written in English, Moored in India." *Bridge-in-Making.* (Spring 2008): 40-43.

Rushdie, Salman. *Imaginary Homelands, Essays and Criticism 1981-1991.* 1991. London: Granta Books in collaboration with Penguin, 1992.

Sharma, R.S. "Language, Literature and Metaphor: A Study in Centrality." *Indian Journal of English Studies*, 42 (2004-2005): 59-71.

Singh, Amardeep. Rev. of *The Hungry Tide*, by Amitav Ghosh. *Amardeep's Weblog.* July 25, 2004. July 14, 2009. <http://www.lehigh.edu/~amsp/2004/08/short-review-of-amitav-ghoshs-hungry.html>.

3

Maternal Bonds: The Celebration of Black Motherhood in Gloria Naylor's *The Women of Brewster Place* and Toni Morrison's *The Bluest Eye*

Anurag Kumar and *Nagendra Kumar*

Portrayal of motherhood has always been one of the most dominant preoccupations of all the Black women writers and finds its vivid and graphic manifestation in their works. These writers build upon black women's experience of and perspectives on motherhood to develop a view of black motherhood in terms of both maternal identity and maternal role. Their perception of motherhood is radically different from that of dominant culture where Black motherhood has been used as a distinctly complex ideology to control Black women. They have been assigned certain stereotypes as breeder, concubine, sapphire, mammy, and mule and projected as more eager for motherhood than their white counterparts in most of white literature. Furthermore, the white literature also endorses their capability as mothers as compared to the white women:

> ...all black women became superhuman mothers, not only for their own people, but for white people as well. More than white woman, it is assured, black women look to motherhood as their chief justification in life; and more than white women, they are physically and emotionally capable of handling the responsibilities with it. (Wade-Gayles, 1984: 59)

The Black women novelists, on the other hand, deal with experience of motherhood rather than the image of it. African American authors have given vibrant portraits of what a mother is and what the act of mothering could be. Motherhood in their view, is fundamentally and profoundly an act of resistance, essential and integral to black women's fight against racism. They also prove that the state of black motherhood has more depth than any other stereotype. The power of motherhood and the empowerment of mothering are what make possible the better world they seek for themselves and their children. Maya Angelou's cycles of autobiographical works, for example, make important contributions to the literary record of black motherhood. Her autobiographies are an important record of how black mothers affect their families and communities.

This paper is a celebration of African American women's resistance and resilience as mothers. It further illustrates how black women writers have deconstructed motherhood as an experience in itself and focuses on the value given to motherhood by these women:

> Black women have...brought into the literature a special knowledge of their lives and experiences that is...different from the descriptions/portrayals of women by men.... They (Black women writers) freed themselves from the roles assigned to them in the writings of their male counterparts, where, depicted as queens and princess, or as earth mothers and idealized Big Mommas of superhuman wisdom and strength, they were unrecognizable as individuals. (Henderson, 1984: XXIV)

Barbara Christian in one of her essays, "An Angle of Seeing: Motherhood in Buchi Emecheta's *Joys of Motherhood* and *Alice Walker's Meridian* (1984)" from her book, *Black Feminist Criticism* (1985) has compared the perception of motherhood in African and African American cultures and has found that though certain societies in Africa are matrilineal but only in letters and not in spirit. Certainly they are valued as mothers, yet their motherhood does not put them in special esteem when they are elderly. Their value as mothers largely exists because they have sons and subsequently that they allow men's names to have a continued link to the next generations. Christian shows that the African American women have moved from being 'un-free' to control their own reproductive experiences. She further puts that motherhood is more than a 'function' of the women. She asserts that motherhood is an entire state of being. Mothering is not restricted to the definition imposed by male or other dominant societies, but is defined by those who are the protectors and nurturers of the children they bear. Paula Gallant Eckard in her book, *Maternal Body and Voices in Toni Morrison, Bobbie Ann, and Lee Smith*, celebrates a paradigm shift in American fiction that marks significant departure from that of patriarchal orientation. She exclusively deals with the works of three 20th century women writers—Toni Morrison, Bobbie Ann, and Lee Smith who portray maternal experiences in their works. In *Toni Morrison and Motherhood: A Politics of the Heart*, Andrea O'Reilly has brilliantly explored the complexities of motherhood and mothering in Morrison's novels from *The Bluest Eye* to *Paradise.* She has co-related the experience of motherhood with their struggle against racism and sexism and their resistance to oppression.

In creating intense mother figure in fiction African American writers have paid tribute to the beauty, struggles, and sorrows of black motherhood. These imagined and real mothers provide an important counter to the negative images of black womanhood circulated in other media. Most of the times abandoned, sometimes separated by socio-cultural factors, the black woman has struggled and survived on her own supporting her children. She could have succumbed but maternal bonds hold her. She looks at her children for every possible emotional support. For the purpose of study the roles of Pauline Breedlove in Toni Morrison's *The Bluest Eye* and Mattie Michael, Cora Lee, and Ciel in Gloria Naylor's *The Women of Brewster Place* as mothers have been chosen.

In *The Bluest Eye,* Morrison presents several aspects of the Black mother. Pauline Breedlove, the crippled mother of Pecola and Tommy, is one of the negative figures in the novel. Her negative feelings towards her children are a result of her inability to adequately provide for them. She feels more comfortable in the luxurious home of her white employer, so she ignores her own culture and her family which results in Pecola's madness. Contrary to it is set a strong mother-daughter bond between Claudia and Mrs. MacTeer. Like Pauline, she is poverty-stricken and has harsh conditions in her life which sometime shape Mrs. MacTeer's rough and cruel treatment of her children. Yet she has come to terms with her situation rather than becoming bitter like Pauline. She is a very loving and understanding mother who realizes the value of motherhood. When in the opening of the novel, Claudia is vomiting, Mrs. MacTeer scolds her but she also remembers her mother's love, "Love, thick and dark as Alaga syrup, eased up into that cracked window. I could smell it—taste it—sweet, musty, with an edge of wintergreen in its base—everywhere in that house" (Morrison, 12). Claudia, unlike Pecola, experiences a moment of union with her mother: "so when I think of autumn, I think of somebody with hands who does not want me to die" (12).

If observed closely, it comes out that the economic oppression of Black mother results in the suffering of her child. The mother is unable to give care and attention to her child during the day because she has to work out side; hence, the child is neglected. Pauline is employed as a housekeeper for a white family. It is her job that finances the major part of her family's living expenses. Family's economic situation prevents them from enjoying a comfortable position in society. On the other side, she is also abused by her spouse, which also affects her relationship with the children. Yet another reason for Pauline unwilling as mother is the life experiences of her own mother where her motherhood had brought only more work and no gratification. She, therefore, escapes into the world of fantasy and experiences vicarious pleasure in identifying herself with white women in the movies.

Another point of focus for Morrison is that Black children are subjected to racism. Since parents are incapable of shielding their children from the racism and violence of the outside world most of the times they surrender which is the case with Pauline. She fails to nurture the feeling of self worth in Pecola because of the lack of self esteem in herself which further results in her dissatisfaction as a mother and feeling of motherhood as a burden. She buries her motherhood deep in her heart and never allows it to come out throughout the novel. If you go deep you find that Pauline herself has not been given proper care and attention in her childhood. Pauline was totally ignored by her parents and she blames their parental neglect on her limp foot. Very early in her life she was introduced to the traditional duties of a woman, like babysitting, which she performs efficiently.

Because of racist stereotyping Black mothers are denied the attention and respect enjoyed by white mothers. Pauline's experience at the maternity hospital has been bad. She recounts the hospital incident prior to the birth of Pecola when the white doctors attending on her comment: "They deliver right away and with no pain. Just like horses" (Morrison, 1979: 97). The racism that controls every other aspect of the Black mother's life and her relationship with her family even dictates whether or not she is capable of feeling pain. Anger on such a comment is diverted towards her children. Pecola becomes the victim of her anger. One more thing adds to her disillusionment is that like her mother, Pecola too, believes in the white standards of beauty. There is a distortion in the natural self of Pauline because she exchanges her role of an ideal mother with that of an ideal servant. It is interesting to note that Black mother's assessment of her condition gives first consideration to her relationship with the racist whites.

Morrison's narrator suggests that there existed a void in Pecola's psyche of a mother which is reflected in where, "Pecola, like Sammy and Cholly always called her mother Mrs. Breedlove" (Morrison, 43). A close reading of the novel shows that Pecola and Mrs. Breedlove never enjoyed a normal mother-daughter relationship as such. There may be one reason as Mrs. Breedlove, throughout the novel has never been able to show maternal love to her. Instead, she has practiced force and violence on Pecola. There is one incident when at her white employer's kitchen, Mrs. Breedlove strikes out on her for spilling the blueberry pie on the floor. It is the refusal of maternal love that leads Pecola to find out love in outside world where she started fantasizing about Shirley Temple. And in the absence of a mother figure, Shirley Temple assumes a maternal image for Pecola.

While Morrison's Pauline diverts her economic frustrations and negligence by her parents towards her children, Gloria Naylor's Mattie Michael in *The Women of Brewster Place* (1982) compensates for her losses by investing heart and soul in Basil. Leaving her parental home and nowhere to go, "she realized that now this (baby) was all she would ever have" (Naylor, 22).

Though Mattie has lost the care and love of her real mother, once she leaves her parental home, she gets the alternate in Miss Eva. Mattie soon comes to think of Miss Eva as a second mother. This relationship of mother daughter gives the bond between the women more and more strength. Gradually both of them become part and parcel of each other's life. Whenever Miss Eva mentions her death in the mock fight, Mattie becomes restless as she "did not want to imagine facing the loss of another mother" (39). Even on their first meeting, both of them start sharing their experiences with each other as if they know each other for years. Mattie behaves like she is talking to her own mother as:

> Miss Eva unfolded her own life and secret exploits to Mattie, and without realizing she was being questioned, Mattie found herself talking about things that she had buried within her. The young black woman and the old yellow woman sat in the kitchen for hours, blending their lives so that what lay behind one and ahead of the other because indistinguishable. (34)

The reason of the bond between these women is perhaps that both of them are subjected to patriarchy when they try to control their sexuality and act on their own will. When Miss Eva tells her story it's almost the same as that of Mattie's: "Child, I know what you talkin' about. My daddy was just like that, too. I remember the night I ran off with my first husband, who was a singer. My daddy hunted us down for three months and then drug me home and kept me lock in my room for weeks with the windows all nailed up. But soon as he let me out, Virgil came back and got me, and we was off again" (34).

So far as the maternal bond between Mattie and Ciel is concerned, its roots are very deep and go back to the time when both of them were happily living in Miss Eva's home. Though they belong to different generations, they rely upon each other. Ciel is portrayed as a child who "looks at Mattie for knowledge and wisdom about how to handle situations in her life. She values Mattie's experience and often looks to her for motherly approval" (Khay).

Serena's death comes up as a blow in Ciel's life. She is completely broken with the pain and grief and gives up the desire to live anymore. At this time in such a critical condition she needs a motherly care and support, Mattie with a strong impulse to protect, "like a Black Brahman cow desperate to protect her young, she surged into the room, pushing the neighboring woman and others out of way" (Naylor, 103) comes to her support. Her love for Ciel comes out when she rocks Ciel literally back to life and gets her to release the pain that she has been holding inside:

> And she rocked...Ciel moaned. Mattie rocked. Propelled by the sound, Mattie rocked her out of bed, out of that room, into a blue vastness just underneath the sun and above time.... She rocked her into childhood and let her see murdered dreams. And she rocked her back, back into the womb, to the nadir of her hurt, and they found it—a slight silver splinter, embedded just below the surface of the skin. And Mattie rocked and pulled—and the splinter gave way, but its roots were deep, gigantic, ragged and they tore up flesh with bits of fat and muscle tissue clinging to them. They left a huge hole, which has already starting to pus over, but Mattie was satisfied. It would heal. (103-04)

Mattie gives her a healing bath which is followed by the tears in Ciel's eyes: "The tears were flowing so freely now Ciel could not see and she allowed herself to be led as if blind"

(105). "And Ciel lay down and cried. But Mattie knew the tears would end. And she would sleep. And morning would come" (105). Mattie does that in order to negate "the psychological destructive effects of temporality, the cycle that has led to the almost overwhelming tragedy Ciel now faces" (Montegomery, 91).

There is yet another mother figure, Cora Lee, "...a beleaguered welfare mother whose love of babies makes her easy prey for male 'shadows' and leaves her with a boisterous brood to clothe, food, and school" (Smith, 270). She is like Pauline who ignores her children and there are only economic reasons behind that. She is alone and has to look after around half a dozen children. Her life is falling apart because of her attitude towards her life and children. It is Kiswana who comes up as a breath of fresh air in her life and kindles self-confidence in her by inviting her and her children to the black performance of *A Midsummer Night's Dream* and, thus, providing the aesthetic satisfaction to fill the vacuum in her life.

Kiswana through the device of the play brings some hope in her saturated life and compels her to rethink her responsibilities towards her children. It is for the first time that Cora realizes how much ragged the clothes of her children are and she is surprised to see all that happened. She takes resolution to check their home work every night, send them to summer school. She also repents as to why "she had beaten him (Sammy) for writing the rhymes on her bathroom walls" (Smith, 1993: 127). Now she could dream about her children in "good jobs in insurance companies and the post office, even doctors or lawyers" (125-26).

In absence of a Kiswana, unlike Cora Lee, Pauline is a negligent mother who fails to give stability and support to her daughter. And in absence of a Mattie, no one is there to heal her as Ciel has been healed. Morrison has depicted her mother-figure as a human being, having all the attributes of a human being who according to the circumstances in which she is placed, responds to the role of motherhood while Naylor takes her mother figures back and connects them to the maternal tradition of Africa where they come to rescue one another.

REFERENCES

Christian, Barbara. *Black Feminist Criticism: Perspectives on Black Women Writers.* Pergamon Press: New York, 1985.

Eckard, Paula Gallant. *Maternal Body and Voices in Toni Morrison, Bobbie Ann, and Lee Smith.* Columbia: University of Missouri Press, 2002.

Henderson, Stephen E. "Introduction." In Evans: xxiii-xxvii, 1984.

Khay. "The Ties that Bind: Female Relationships in the Works of Gloria Naylor". December 6, 2006. www.associatedocument.com

Montgomery, Maxine Lavon. *The Apocalypse in African-American Fiction.* University Press of Florida, U.S., 1996.

Morrison, Toni. *The Bluest Eye.* London: Chatto and Windus Limited, 1979.

Naylor, Gloria. *The Women of Brewster Place.* New York: Viking, 1982. Paperback reprint, New York: Penguin, 1983.

O'Reilly, Andrea. *Toni Morrison and Motherhood: A Politics of the Heart.* Albany: State University of New York Press, 2004.

Smith, Valerie, Bachilek, Lea and Litz, Walton A. *African American Writers Profiles of Their Lives and Works.* MacMillan Pub. Co., New York, 1993.

Wade-Gayles, Gloria. "No Crystal Stair: Visions of Race and Sex in Black Women's Fiction". New York: Pilgrim Press, 1984.

4

Rushdie and Naipaul: India and Their Non-Fiction

Jaya Kapoor

Naipaul and Rushdie are two of the earliest Indian writers in English who found recognition and acceptance and paved the way for so many other writers to follow. It is not easy to do what Naipaul and Rushdie did—to make a self obsessed colonial mindset sit up and take note of the work being done by writers from once colonized countries. They wrote in the language of the colonizers making them accessible to the western audience while talking about the third world countries. Both Rushdie and Naipaul have gained status of icons and examples for writers of the younger generation in Indian literature in English.

The question I would like to explore in the paper explores the extent to which the two writers can be considered to be examples for such young writers in India. The reason I take up their non-fiction is that this is where we need to go if we are to look for the way a writer identifies himself and the position he places himself in within a literary tradition. There is no question about the contribution of both Naipaul and Rushdie to the changes that the novel saw after their emergence both in terms of style and content. The idea to be explored is whether Indian writing in English needs to be directed towards the western or international reader, or towards the Indian reader. In the world today it is not that a writer will not reach out to readers beyond the country or even to readers in other languages, especially if they are writing in a language with an international reach like English. But the writer has to be rooted in a certain literary tradition and deal with an environment in his writings. That is where we need to look at their non-fiction and to question the authority of the two stalwarts. Any honest analysis of their work will accept that they belong to the western literary traditions and address a western reader. Then how can they become a part of the Indian literary scene. The argument can be raised that they are Diasporic writers. Indian Diasporic writing is today a substantial body of work and it is high time we started looking at the parameters by which to judge them. Their experiences are bound to be different from those of the Indian writer living in India. But if they wish to be called Indian writers in English there should be something more Indian in their writings than the names of the characters or the decaying social-personal value systems. Both Naipaul and Rushdie have tie and again been questioned on both accounts. If their engagement with India and its related issues is like a western intellectual why should they not be considered as such instead of the spokesmen for India as they are taken to be. The diasporic writers coming after them find it easy to follow them but if we are to build a vibrant tradition of Indian writing in English we must now start judging writers from criterion more than the sales figures in the country and the international markets. And the diaspora of India is not one monolithic body. Let us first try to understand the Indian diaspora and try to place its writing within the ambit of Indian writing in English.

Makrand Paranjape talks of two categories of Diaspora—one where the migration happened pre-liberalization, possibly in the early days of colonization where the migrants were taken as indentured laborers and the other which went in search of better opportunities by their own choice. For the first type, leaving the homeland was a compulsion and there was no coming back. The places where they went were not of their choice and they were subject to the same exploitation there that they had been back home and also had to deal with an alien culture and language that made no attempt to assimilate them so that they kept their homeland alive in small symbols and rituals which they followed rigorously as a part of their identity. Naipaul gives a picture of the Indians in similar tones when he recollects his childhood days and says that the Indian community was a closed community that strove to keep India alive by following the rituals and routines of the homeland—

> ...with their blinkered view of the world they were able to recreate eastern Uttar Pradesh or Bihar wherever they went....to leave India's sacred soil, to cross the "black water," was considered an act of self defilement. So completely did these migrants recreate India in Trinidad that they imposed a similar restriction on those who wished to leave Trinidad. (Naipaul, 2003: 43)

The other category are the migrants who went away because they felt that they had better opportunities outside than at home. These people usually went into a system where they could be better adjusted probably even assimilated and build identities for themselves relatively independent of their home culture. Paranjape places Naipaul in the first category and Rushdie in the second and then corrects himself and says that Naipaul belonged more in the second category since it was his father who had to face the identity challenges of displacement and colonialism while he himself had moved out to England and found tools to forge an identity for himself.

But both of them have been rather skeptically received when it comes to being spokesmen for their homeland. In their non-fictional works the way these writers have talked about their homeland especially because they are hailed as writers of Indian origin and also like to project themselves as such. As people of Indian origin they don't belong to the mainstream of the world they are geographically located in—the European and American tradition give them acceptance as writers of Indian origin putting a compulsion on them to talk about the land that is increasingly catching the attention of the western literary world. And being located outside India and having not been exposed to the country except for occasional visits, they are also not taken to be in the thick of the things and belonging at home. What is very fascinating is that they accept the life of the margins and don't even think of coming back to the land whose voice they are labelled.

Makrand Paranjape while analysing of South Asian Canadian Literature quotes Victor Ramraj—as saying that diasporic writings are concerned with individual's yearning f or the homeland and countered by a yearning to belong to the current place of abode—and observes that this makes the diasporic narratives both transitional and liminal. The texts themselves are journeys between source cultures and target cultures, between homelands and diasporas, until the two overlap, change places, or merge (Paranjape, 2001: 163) and Shiva Kumar almost reflects the idea while talking about Naipaul for whom diasporas matter because they give the people a chance to get away, to enact a radical form of cultural exogamy, to rethink the very idea of culture (63).

The problem with Naipaul was that he could not place himself fully within the history of Trinidad, he was too acutely aware of his Indian roots to do so. Time and again in his discussions and essays he sounds acutely conscious of the fact that that the Indians in Trinidad lived a life that was not a part of their present reality but a memory of a lost past. They could not integrate with the local culture and had begun to loose the roots that they had brought with them. Another drawback with the people was that most of the people who had gone to Trinidad were poor and uneducated for whom culture had been a lifestyle and a geographical location. With their displacement they brought the rituals but the meaning of the rituals was lost. He talks of the Dussehra celebrations and how he could not make sense of the festival since it is primarily a festival associated with crops and season change which meant nothing in Trinidad. Slowly he also realized that he had lost the memories of the language that India spoke—the language of the culture and mindset. He was conscious of India but the India he had been told about in his childhood was different from the present India he saw and not having been exposed to the growth of the country first hand, there was a gap between his idea of India and the India he saw.

> I grew up with two ideas of history, almost two ideas of time. There was history with dates...(there) was a time beyond recall, mythical...beyond(and sometimes even within) people's memories was undated time, historical darkness. Out of this darkness (extending to place as well as to time) we had all come. The India where Gandhi and Nehru operated was historical and real. The India from which we had come was impossibly remote, almost as imaginary as the land of Ramayana, our Hindu epic. (Naipaul, 2003: 89)

Chinua Achabe said about Naipaul that although Naipaul was writing about Africa, he was not writing for Africans. The reason could probably be that he existed in a state of rootlessness though he tried to call it cosmopolitan. His Indian connection dissolved in his early childhood. He says,

> ...the Indians (in Trinidad) endured and prospered. The India they recreated was allowed to survive. It was an India in which a revolution had occurred. It was an India in isolation, unsupported...soon India could be seen to be no more than a habit, a self-imposed psychological restraint, wearing thinner with the years. (43)

The roots of a writer are the raw material he can use to create his world and as Nirmal Verma puts it—a modern indian writer can still hear, if he wishes to, what Virginia Woolf called "an echo from the past". These echoes being were not easy for a person like Naipaul to hear because not only had his people left and lost the memories of these voices but he had moved away from these people as well to the West where the echoes from the past did not resonate with his own memories and identity. He admits to being isolated "Great novelists wrote about highly organized societies. I had no such society...no writer, however individual his vision, could be separated from his society" (x). He is not talking about the Trinidadian society so much as the Indian part of it that he had been a part of.

Rushdie is more fortunate in that he could relate to the land and its identity better but his problem was that he was unwilling to honestly reflect these echoes in his works. He preferred to call himself an exile and talked of imaginary homelands when he only had to turn inwards to find the roots that he talked of yearning for. But for some reason he refuses took inwards deep and long enough to find these roots. He chooses instead to almost scan the surface and find random memories to tell stories that look like tales of a fantastic India but in fact have nothing of the country in them. And in return he takes the right to express his vision of the country. For instance, Rushdie is highly critical of the change in the name of Bombay to Mumbai and said during a discussion on the recent terror attacks on the city,

> It is Bombay that was attacked and not Mumbai. And, by the way, I cannot say, and this is the only time I will say it, the words "Chhatrapati Shivaji Terminus". This railway station is and always will be VT. And so, because these are the names of love, the others are the artificial names imposed by the politicians. But these are the names of the city that we love. (*The Outlook*, 19 Dec. 2008)

To constantly look over the shoulder and live in the past are very symptomatic of a diasporic writer as, in "imaginary homelands" to put it in Rushdie's own terms. So why does it matter?—It matters especially in a country like India with a civilization going unbroken for at least three thousand years is explained by Nirmal Verma when he ponders on the changes that came in the country over time,

> Indeed, distortion is the price history seems to have exacted from Indian civilization in order to give it a breathing space for survival. In fact, the distorted surface is so inextricably fused with the original texture that it seems impossible to disentangle one from the other...if one gets obsessed only by the stains and scars of a culture, one would see nothing of the truth and tenacity of the original material. (Verma, 2000: 146)

Rushdie is not wrong in looking back wistfully at the past but then the question will be raised that which past are we to go back to? For some the names that Rushdie finds connectedness to are painful reminders of a colonial rule. It becomes not a question of denying history but finding a history apart from what the colonial masters told us. That might be a glorious past of the West when they ruled the world but we might not want to celebrate that phase of our past. The texture of the Indian civilization has seen such changes and survived them is something that Rushdie does not seem to appreciate. He looks at the country as an Western Expert on India and not as an Indian. His views in "Step Across This Line" have beautiful personal memories of the country but nothing that could tell about the pride he takes in being an Indian. He sounds worried about the politicians and about the corruption and about the communalism and then regrets the apparent unconcern of the common man with the celebration of Fifty years of Independence. But then changes track and talks about frontierless nations and they ask to beware of the writer who sets himself up to be the voice of a nation. He mentions Naipaul as a deliberately uprooted intellectual while the other kind he says is the intellectual uprooted against his will. "There is great loss, and much yearning, in such rootlessness. But there is also gain" (Rushdie, 2003: 67). The writer gains no doubt, but how do we combine this refusal to belong, to be rooted, with a wish to be looked upon as an Indian writer.

In their fictional world their perspectives about India are camouflaged by the layers of imagination but in their non-fiction their conflict shows through more visibly. Both Naipaul and Rushdie spent years at prestigious universities in Europe that shaped their minds and gave them the tools that they used as writers. Their writings are a product of their grooming and not their roots and more than the fiction their non-fiction reveals that they cater to and address the land of their location and not of their roots. Being writers of Indian origin proved to be a an advantage to them at a time when the interest in the country as a land where fantastic met the tragic was beginning. They became spokesmen for a world they had precious little ties left with. Their greatest advantage was that they spoke in the language the West understood, using the tools that the West had found acceptable and were located in the U.S. and the U.K. where they could be heard loud and clear. But these are the very basis of objections raised while questioning their acceptability as spokesmen for the subcontinent. Tabish Khair says about the acceptance that has come for both Rushdie and Naipaul "they belong to a tradition that is less uncomfortable for the cultured Western reader and critic to face up to. If they present difference, they present just a different aspect of the West" (*The Hindu*, Sept. 14, 2009).

And having been handed the mikes to speak they found themselves short of the depth of understanding and took populist stance that more or less confirmed the West's idea of the country leading to applause and recognition. Nirmal Verma talks about the responsibilities of being a modern Indian writer,

> ...to be a truly modern Indian writer—to be modern and Indian at the same time—demands an immense imaginative effort. It demands that the writer enters into the central stream of a civilization which, though distorted here and disrupted there, has been able to preserve its flow during the last three thousand years. (Verma, 2000: 147)

Naipaul fails to place himself within the Indian tradition and though he is an observer with the tag of an insider, it would be inappropriate to call him an Indian writer if we agree with Verma's criterion. Naipaul does see the fault lines that have developed in the body of Indian culture but these fault lines are inevitable and probably they will be better understood if we take the culture to be a flux and not a composite body.

The trilogy that Naipaul wrote could perhaps be better understood if they are taken not as documentaries about the country but rather a process of Naipaul's understanding of the country. Looking from the perspective of a western mind, Naipaul found it hard to come to terms with the picture of contrasts that the country presented, but gradually as he started coming to a relatively more balanced point of view or rather when the country became more accessible to him he could understand the language of the country better and found a million mutinies here. Those mutinies that he saw in his trilogy could not have happened overnight, did not happen overnight, only he discovered them then.

The question arises then, that how far are the two writers to be considered representative of Indian literature or even of Indian literature in English? There is need to look at the question deeply now because unlike a few years back when the entire body of Indian literature in English comprised of a handful of writers, and moreover the readership was within a very limited range, now there is an appreciable increase on both accounts. So writers of the stature of Rushdie and Naipaul provide role models for the new generation. They might not be willing to accept the responsibility but by the mere act of acknowledging their Indianness they become a part of the tradition and must accept the responsibility of the role. The idea of tradition that Eliot talked about and that Nirmal Verma tries to analyze is not without validity. The idea of rootlessness and frontierless world that both these writers talk about, finally have to identify with some tradition. To talk of such Indian tradition might lead to a sounding like a plea for Nativism, but the point I wish to raise here is not about Nativism it is not even about voicing the concern of the subaltern. Nativism leads to viewing the past as a composite whole and denies literature room for movement for the flux that would lead to a vibrant and growing literature. The subaltern again identifies with one phase of the past tying it down and inhibiting independent movement. In both cases both Rushdie and Naipaul are right in not acknowledging a tradition. But now the question is that how far should we be cautious in approaching them both as Indian writers? The answer is probably very cautious because both the writers refuse to belong where they come from and are labelled outsiders where they are. Naipaul's writings are about rootlessness while Rushdie's about hybridity. They don't exist in a tradition and refuse to exist in one. As individual writers they may be right but then how are they to be included in the tradition of Indian writing in English? How are they to provide models for a tradition of Indian Writing in English.

The idea is not to stop fighting the tradition nor to wholly succumb to it. A writer who comes to mind at this point is Tagore. Tagore achieved fame from his translated *Gitanjali* which does not measure up to the standard of the original Bangla text. Tagore as a musician and theatre artist contributed much to Indian Literature and art but even in India we prefer to study and discuss Tagore the poet of *Gitanjali*. In missing the other aspects of his genius in theatre and music where he brought some radical shifts in tradition and still maintained the essential Indianness of the spirit we lose a vital link to the movement of Indian literary tradition towards modernity. We typecast him in a way. A similar argument is raised by Prasanna when he talks about tradition,

> ...In India tradition is too heavy on us especially on creative people, especially on intellectuals, and how do you comprehend the tradition? You can only comprehend it by fighting it...let us not think that Indian tradition is simply going to vanish, simply because a writer fights it here or a writer fights it there. A whole lot of writers and artists have fought it and made it richer. (*Nativism*, 98)

To fight a tradition you need to understand its strengths and weaknesses and then have a roadmap for the changes you wish to see in the tradition. Neither Naipaul nor Rushdie wrote with even a remote idea Indian writing in English tradition in mind. Naipaul admits to the trauma he felt at the lack of roots and cultural identity and perhaps his writings reflect this trauma again and again. Rushdie, on the other hand, willingly gave up such roots to celebrate hybridity in his writings. But does Indian literature in English stand to gain a direction and standards from such ambivalent positions? Their non-fiction shows that they are engaged with the idea of India constantly even apart from their fiction. But their views do not show any inclination to be engaged with the tradition of literature in the country. Shashi Tharoor views this colossal proliferation of books about India in the foreign bookstores as an "indication of mounting international interest in India"

(Tharoor, 1997). Or could it be a sudden consciousness of the vast market for such international books in India?

The writer who comes to mind here is Agha Shahid Ali. He was a writer who wrote in English, lived in the U.S. but on reading his poetry there is no doubt about the fact that his poetry enriches the Indian Poetry in English even while talking about his immediate physical locations and experiences. His experiments of writing Gazals in English were a success because he understood not only the technique of the form but also the cultural connotations that underline the form and give it identity. His concern with Kashmir went beyond a comment on terrorism or the inability of the system to handle the problem. It understood the problem as not just a law and order problem but as a threat to the fabric of the unique Kashmiri culture. Should we not demand a similar depth of vision from the other writers of Indian origin? What changes should merely be the language of expression and not the entire mindset and commitment.

So the idea must not be not to belong but rather to enrich. And neither Naipaul nor Rushdie seem to admit to an attempt to enrich the Indian tradition, to speak from within the system. Both Rushdie and Naipaul are a product of the Western system and address an audience that is primarily Western. Their ideas about India are best taken as those of such intellectuals instead of an Indian writer. If we approach them with an idea of finding a direction for Indian writing in English we are probably knocking at the wrong doors. We need to find writers who are aware of the demands of Indian literary tradition and integrate Indian writing in English with that tradition instead of blindly calling glamorous faces of international publishing business as Indian writing in English.

WORKS CITED

Naipaul, V.S., *Literary Occasions*, London: Picador, 2003.

Paranjape, Makarand, Introduction, Indiaspora, ed. Makarand Paranjape, Delhi: Indialog Publications, 2001.

Prasanna, "A Critique of Nativism in Contemporary Indian Theatre", *Nativism: Essays in Criticism*, ed. Makarand Paranjape, New Delhi: Sahitya Akademi, 1997.

Rushdie, Salaman, *Step Across This Line*, London: Vintage, 2003.

Tharoor, Shashi, *India: From Midnight to the Millennium and Beyond*, New Delhi: Penguin, 2007.

Verma, Nirmal, *India And Europe: Selected Essays*, ed. Nirmal Verma, Simla: IIAS Simla, 2000.

Online sources

www.outlookindia.com.

www.thehindu.com.

5

Situating Diaspora: A Comparative Study of *The Namesake* and *The Inheritance of Loss*

R.N. Rai and *Ashutosh Singh*

Prevailing complexities and diversities of the 'human reality' have compelled contemporary thinking to interrogate and deconstruct given concepts like 'home', 'abroad', 'nation', 'culture', and others in both 'worldly' and 'textual' contexts. In postcolonial studies diaspora culture in all its potency of migrancy, hybridity and cross-cultural ambivalence has come to acquire a vital significance since it demonstrates that culture need not remain a temporally or spatially closed and fixed notion but can well be fluid and mobile. Stuart Hall explains that diasporan culture demonstrates that identity is not a thing given, but something always in the process of being asserted The interaction and commingling of various cultures certainly open new routes and modes of thinking about the individual and group identities of Diasporas, and help them to outgrow the stereotyped experiences of uprootedness, displacement and marginalization (236).

Both Jhumpa Lahiri and Kiran Desai belong to the second generation expatriate writers and deal with the manifestations and consequences of different aspects of diaspora. Jhumpa Lahiri, the 2000 Pulitzer Prize winner for her collection of short stories entitled the *Interpreter of Maladies* has created a specific niche for herself in the literary arena of Indian English fiction with her debut novel *The Namesake*. This novel is diasporic in consciousness and deals with the issues of adaptation, adjustment and accommodation in a world where the boundaries are thinned or often blurred. Her novel brings to the fore many of the issues that Indians, settled in the promising land of opportunities, face in America. The narrative revolves round the problems faced by a couple (i.e. Ashoke and Ashima) in a different country—the clash of cultures, the relationship between parents and children, the generation gap and identity crisis etc. Kiran Desai being a modern expatriate Indian novelist, had herself experienced displacement, dislocation and cultural clash. In her novel she writes of the cultural hybridity of the post-colonial migrant and the expatriate condition of hybridity. Her novel *The Inheritance of Loss* which won the 2006 Man Booker prize, deals with her own situation of migrancy, expatriation and alienation from the mother country. The paper is divided into two parts, the first part deals with *The Namesake* in the light of diasporic consciousness and the second part seeks to critically examine Kiran Desai's *The Inheritance of Loss* in terms of representation of individual and cultural identity of Indians with reference to their diasporic situatedness.

I

As a diasporic writer, Jhumpa Lahiri deals with multi-cultural society—partly from 'inside' and partly from 'outside'. She strives for her native identity and simultaneously endeavours to evolve a new identity in adopted Anglo-American cultural landscape. However, in this clash of cultures, she faces an immigrant's dislocation and displacement. She regards dislocation as a permanent condition of human existence. Hence her sense of belonging to a particular place and culture and at the same time being an 'outsider' to it creates an inner tension in her characters.

Lahiri in her novel, *The Namesake* acts as a dispassionate narrator visiting the private limited spaces of Bengali immigrants in America, a world which is without an axis, collapsible, deceptive, where the state of exile is a cultural as well as an emotional denial. Familiar diasporic themes—the uneasy status of the developed world and India and tension between family tradition and individual freedom form part of her novel. Its theme centres round the story of Gogol, named after the Russian writer Nikolai Gogol. Struggling to come to terms with his expatriate situation, Gogol experiences all the ambivalence of his parents (Ashoke and Ashima) who have not yet been able to be assimilated into the new land. A constant combination of distance and intimacy binds them to their native city of Calcutta which of Lahiri seems to be a vast, unruly, fascinating city. They have no home at Calcutta, yet they insist on calling that city their home. Ashoke and Ashima Ganguli and their world are constantly juggling past, present and future. Their experiences are different and so are their reactions as well as expectations. After the death of her husband, Ashima decides to spend six months of the year in the America and six in India. In spite of her feeling of displacement, marginality and a crisis of identity, this move is directed towards finding new ways of adaptation into a new country. And after divorce from Gogol, Moushmi goes to live with Dimitri and plans to leave for Paris "immersing herself in a third language, a third culture" (214). In an extended sense it reveals the emergence of the multicultural and global identity of the second generation immigrants. Thus Jhumpa can be categorized as a multi-cultural, diasporic, post-colonial, marginal, South-Asian woman writer. As a second generation expatriate, Jhumpa stands at an interesting border as well as the cross-roads of culture. As a part of the margin, she is a force that has in the US always broadened the mainstream. The home that the parents left behind is no longer the home for the second generation and hence she faces a greater problem with fixity in space hardly possible, and an identity which seems elusive, with attempts to transcend marginalization by bridging the gap between the centre and margin. Like most expatriate writers she realizes that she can portray only what she has experienced. As said by Subhendu Mund, "For various reasons, the present diaspora tends to alienate the immigrants from their roots in spite of themselves, compelling them to live between two worlds: the imaginary and the real, the past and the present, and the virtual and the material" (108).

Diasporic Indian is like the banyan tree, the traditional symbol of the Indian way of life, he spreads out his roots in several soils, drawing nourishment from one when the rest dry up. Far from being homeless, he has several homes, and that is the only way he has increasingly come to feel at home in the world. It is not that the centre has shifted; only the margins have expanded to push the home culture further to outer space. Children of Indian families born in US seem to adapt more easily to western society, despite resistance from parents. This, of course, causes an inevitable gap between parents and children. Gogol does not accept his father's chose of his name. He thinks that "names die over time, that they perish just as people do" (70). He keeps his relationship with Ruth and Maxine and flirts with them knowing that his parents do not support this cultural deviation. While Ashima takes long to recover after her husband's death, Gogol's girlfriend Maxine does not understand the intensity of her shock; she rather laughs at her as Gogol in his childhood had laughed at the sight of his father's shaving off his hair with a grief-stricken heart after his grandfather's death in India. When we fail to understand the motive and emotion that a culture carries, it appears strange and hence incites laughter. This results in a certain type of ambivalence among parents about how to cope with and continuously modify their traditional value systems. Immigrant parents perceive the real pressure of westernization in some sensitive areas such as their children's associations with the opposite sex, and the issues of dating and marriage, which conflict with the traditional Indian method of match-making. Lahiri precisely portrays the children of Ashoke and Ashima as perfectly American. Gogol dates with one after the other girl and Sonia dates with an American. Ashoke and Ashima have no choice but to be quiet. Gogol enjoys premarital sex with Ruth. But his parents have not expressed any curiosity about his girlfriend. Theirs is a kind of lukewarm response, and indifferent attitude towards that incident as the text shows, "His relationship with her is one accomplishment in his life about which they are not in the least proud or pleased" (116). When at last Ashoke and Ashima do give a piece of their mind to Gogol, the latter says that "marriage is the last thing on his mind" (117). Thus their "adherence to a diasporic community is demonstrated by an acceptance of an inescapable link with their past migration history" (ix), says Robert Cohen. It also reveals that migrant Bengalis carry with them their "beliefs, traditions, customs, behaviours, and values" along with their "possessions and belongings to new places" (211) as remarked by John McLeod.

The confrontation between the East and the West, the strange Love-Hate relationship that exists between the two, the cultural alienation and the loss of identity faced by the expatriates and immigrants are some of the aspects that are presented with a deep psychological insight. The novel projects Ashima and Ashoke as cultural survivors in America's multicultural milieu. They demonstrate the lives of hybridity, inbetweenness and liminality. It is difficult for them to maintain cultural insularity, and like millions of immigrant Indians they essentialise their life in cultural milieu of America. But finally it is their contra-acculturation and rooting for India that allows them peace and consolation in moments of catharsis. Lahiri seems to say that more than a mere metaphorical twist, dislocation has now become an inescapable physical and geographical reality. The indigenous Indian values and Western concept of morality, despite conflicting discordant element seems to mingle and reconcile in a peculiar way. Lahiri investigates the life situations of Ashoke, Ashima and Gogol when they are in a state of cross-cultural shock; they feel suffocated and pinned on the wall. In their efforts to know the self, they examine their inner altitudes, analyze their divided being inherited and acquired. Confrontation with other culture means discovery of one's own nation, roots and identity. It is a search for one's reality, an attempt to regain belongingness, in order to get confirmed their affirmation and adaptation towards the ancestry and the identity of their own. Gogol reimagines the locus of his Indian identity whose marriage with Moushmi ends in divorce.

Poornima rightly suggests that "the salvation in the diaspora's disquiet journey in an alien land lies in adopting the assimilationist approach, in unearthing the realities of

American way of life while maintaining bonds with his homeland to replenish his emotional bankruptcy that has come to be his lot" (25). The immigrants always suffer from feelings that there is no single place to which they belong, and it is in this sense Lahiri tries to give a tongue to the feelings of immigrants through the character of Gogol. The identity crisis and what Homi K. Bhabha calls the feeling of "in-betweenness" (1) and belonging "nowhere" is experienced by Gogol who straddles two cultures and suffers from the loss of roots and social dislocation.

Ashoke and Ashima caught between two worlds, one which is dead as they have left it behind and the other which is not yet born as they have not yet accepted it. As Lahiri had herself experienced and it is the common experience of most of the children of expatriate parents, it is difficult for them to answer the question like 'where are you from?'—which are both troubling and enigmatic. As they were born in the US, the answer should be a place in the US (New Jersey, for example) but that does not satisfy the questioner. And the question is repeated 'but, where are you from?' The second-generation expatriate like Lahiri or Gogol in the novel find it difficult, almost impossible, to say 'from India' as they know that country only from occasional visits or from the memories of their parents and the tales constantly recounted by them. They find themselves isolated and insulated (in two separate cultures)—one impregnable culture at home and a totally different one outside. Lahiri's use of two names and hence two identities for the protagonist becomes the perfect metaphor for the diasporic experiences.

II

The Inheritance of Loss has portrayed the various experiences of the diasporas in New York and Kalimpong. Desai's characters confront hardship and despair in an unforgiving world. After being orphaned at a young age, Sai a teenage girl, is living with her retired judge and anglophile grandfather, Jemubhai, and her grandfather's cook. The mid-1980 finds Sai experiencing her first crush, her grandfather feeling tormented by past injustices, and the cook swelling with pride for Biju, a son he misses dearly. The backdrop to the story is the soaring Himalayan peak of Kanchenjunga, so rich in Tibetan mythology. The mountain, viewed from Kalimpong where "India blurred into Bhutan and Sikkim" (9)—is a constant presence in the novel, unchanging throughout the political turmoil of the Nepalese uprising in the late 1980s that forms the context in which Desai constructs her powerful tale of the most enduring legacy of colonialism—loss in all its guises. The other prominent place in the novel is New York City, not the glamorous New York of the movies, but the underbelly of the city, inhabited by illegal immigrants trying to eke out a living in sordid kitchens of dodgy restaurants, always at the mercy of ruthless employers and always on the move, one step in front of the immigration authorities. Relationships in the novel are shaped by reluctantly held family ties, economic imperatives, political upheaval and most significantly, the hybridity and displacement that are key markers of what are frequently termed as the postcolonial condition. The book rejoices the intermingling of cultures: "Above, the restaurant was French, but below in the kitchen it was Mexican and Indian. And, when a Paki was hired, it was Mexican, Indian, Pakistani" (281). Desai describes *The Inheritance of Loss* as a book that, 'tries to capture what it means to live between East and West and what it means to be an immigrant,' and, 'what happens when a Western element is introduced into a country that is not of the West'. Desai aims to describe, "what happens when you take people from a poor country and place them in a wealthy one. How does the imbalance between these two worlds change a person's thinking and feeling? How do these changes manifest themselves in a personal sphere, a political sphere, over time?" As Desai notes, "these are old themes that continue to be relevant in today's world" (www.bookbrowse.com.).

Sai's maternal grandfather Jemubhai, a retired judge, travels as a young student from India to Cambridge to study law. On the strength of being the first boy in the district to go to an English university and assured of a powerful career on his return, he acquires both a large debt from local moneylenders and a 14-year-old bride. His father-in-law arranges for members of a military band to serenade his departure at the Bombay docks. His arrival in England is met with less pomp—he struggles to find a room to let, and when he does find one mile away from the university, his landlady is unwelcoming and insists on calling him "James". Jemu spends his entire time at Cambridge locked in his room, studying fourteen hours a day, eating his landlady's inadequate food and not making any friends. He suffered seriously from loneliness, longing and difference from others in a foreign country:

> For entire days nobody spoke to him at all, his throat jammed with words unuttered, his heart and mind turned into blunt aching things, and elderly ladies, even the hapless—blue-haired, spotted, faces like collapsing pumpkins—moved over when he sat next to them in the bus, so he knew that whatever they had, they were secure in their conviction that it wasn't even remotely as bad as what he had. (39)

He scrapes through his exams, makes it into the Indian Civil Service, and returns to India to serve his Majesty as a magistrate. Having experienced awful dislocation in England, he now finds that he cannot make a place for himself in India—he is too English. He is sent back to India equipped with a snake-bite kit, a twelve-bore shotgun and a tennis racket. Despite a glorious reception, Jemu finds his wife grotesque and his people alien. He rejects her, the baby he just manages to father, his family, their ways and becomes more English than the English—trying and failing to hunt animals with his gun, eating toast for breakfast and crumpets for tea, and pouring all his love into his relationship with his dog. He is a tragic and lonely figure. Damaged unalterably by the experience of being a young man during the British raj is Jemu, the retired judge, now living in a rambling run-down mansion called Cho Oyu built for a Scotsman with romantic notions of Himalayan life in Kalimpong. Sent to England as a young boy by his ambitious father to complete his law degree which he passed only because of the quota system, Jemu wanted nothing more than to be English and, after his return to India, he found himself unable to reconcile himself to being Indian. Robert Cohen describes Diaspora as the communities of people living together in one country who "acknowledge that the old country—a nation often buried in deep in languages, religion, custom or folklore—always has some claim on their loyalty and emotions" (ix). Diasporas thus live in one country as community but look across time and space to another. The migrant Diasporas and their descendents experience displacement, fragmentation, marginalization and discontinuity in the cultural 'discourse' of the subject countries and the respective land. Through the life of Biju, Desai presents the status of the illegal immigrants and the feeling of alienation often experienced by expatriates. Desai being an Indian might have experienced the same anxiety as a foreigner. In her novel there is constant effort to establish identity. Carole Boyce Davies writes: "Migration creates the desire for home, which in turn produces the rewriting of home. Home sickness or homelessness, the rejection of home or the longing for home becomes motivating factors in this rewriting. Home can only have meaning once one experiences a level of displacement from it" (113).

During the analysis of immigration and its associated problems it must be understood that new immigrants come from a society where they had been part of the whole community. Once these people leave their original homelands, they experience the pangs of alienation. The outcome of their deliberate choice is dispossession and displacement. Biju finds himself a foreigner in a world that is constantly in a flux and is devoid of any settled convention, where native rootedness is viewed as backwardness and any allegiance to communal customs is dismissed as superstition. With his poor adaptability and inhibitions inherited from his native culture, Biju continues his search for an elusive home while leading the wretched life of an illegal immigrant in the precarious anonymity of New York's restaurants and basement kitchens: "There was a whole world in the basement kitchens of New York, but Biju was ill-equipped for it" (22). The immigrant has to deal with various types of people who face unfamiliar problems in the foreign country. As the fulfillment of his father's long-cherished dream Biju, "At 4:25 A.M. made his way to Queen of Tarts bakery" (75). "My son works in New York", the cook boasted to everyone he met. "He is the manager of a restaurant business" (84). Biju worked at various restaurants. There were many problems continually faced by Indians in the US. The protagonist is engaged in an effort to get acquainted with the American way of life. Biju hates the people who give up Indian style for hybridized habits. After a long period of pain and humiliation Biju books his return ticket "tired of the greatest loss the can come out from one's family". "Biju stepped out of the airport into the Calcutta night, warm, mammalian. His feet sank into dust winnowed to softness at his feet, and he felt an unbearable feeling, sad and tender, old and sweet like the memory of falling asleep, a baby on his mother's lap" (300). Biju's never ending tale of pain continues; a gang of robbers reaches there and offers a lift in their jeep, they strip him of all his material possession and even his dignity. "Darkness fell and he sat right in the middle of the path without his baggage, without his savings, worst of all without his pride, Back from America with far less than he'd ever had" (317). He reaches the Judge's house as a figure in a night gown, a symbol of the dispossessed.

Desai asserts that India is a land of multiculturalism. She writes about terrorism and introduces the operation of the Gorkha National Liberation Front as a subplot. Gyan, Sai's tutor and lover, is a member of the GNLF. Sai is a product of multiculturalism. She fails to keep the relationship with Gyan who hates western style. The uprooted life of the Judge ends with the fruitless search for his pet dog Mutt. As he has virtually lost his Indian heritage, he fails to find happiness in life. Sai, torn between cultures, remains a dispossessed soul. And Biju finally reaches the home land as the sad metaphor of the Indian diaspora.

Hybridity is definitely a very important subject in Kiran Desai's *The Inheritance of Loss*. The term signifying key concept of cultural diversity in Desai's novel, which stretches from India to New York, analyses the post-colonial and post-modern set up of the expatriate Indian. Mala Pandurang in her article "Loss and Longing" remarks: "This is a story as much of loss as it is of bitter longing for a world that eludes each of the characters, as a consequence of their class backgrounds and postmodern legacies. They thereby become the inheritors of loss" (32). Set in post-colonial India, Kiran Desai's novel *The Inheritance of Loss* vividly highlights a number of issues like globalization, economic inequality, multiculturalism, immigration, racism, terrorism, nationalism and its resulting consequences.

Hence, the diasporic space of Desai seems to be very broad as she is nearly dealing with every aspect of diaspora in her novel. Lahiri on the other hand is mainly concerned with the problems that are being faced by the Bengali immigrants in America. She also focuses on the family relationships, and in Manjeet Inder Singh's terms portrays 'bifocal' and 'bilocal' figures (3). Both writers belong to the second generation of diasporic writing and both have made significant contribution to the growth of fiction writing.

WORKS CITED

Anderson, Benedict. *Imagined Communities*. London: Verso, 1987.

Bhabha, Homi K. *The Location of Culture*. London: Routledge, 1994.

Brah, Avtar. *Cartographies of Diaspora: Contesting Identities*. London: Routledge, 2002.

Cohen, Robert. *Global Diaspora: An Introduction*. UCL. Press, 1997.

Davies, Carole Boyce. *Black Women Writing and Identity Migrations of the Subject*. London: Routledge, 1994.

Desai, Kiran. *The Inheritance of Loss*. London and New Delhi: Penguin Books, 2006.

Hall, Stuart. "Cultural Identity and Diaspora", *Theorizing Diaspora: A Reader*. Eds. Jana Evans Braziel and Anita Mannur. Oxford: Blackwell Publishers, 2003.

Lahiri, Jhumpa. *The Namesake*. New Delhi: Harper Collins Publishers, 2008.

Mc Leod, John. *Beginning Post-Colonialism*, New York: Manchester University Press, 2000.

Mund, Subhendu. "History, Ethnicity and Gender in Female Fiction of the Indian Diaspora". *The Atlantic Review*, Vol. 6, No. 1-2, 2005.

Padurang, Mala. "Loss and Longing." Rev. of *The Inheritance of Loss*. *The Book Review*, Vol. 30, No. 5, May 2006.

Poornima. "Changing Patterns of Human Relationships in Jhumpa Lahiri's *The Namesake.*" Ed. Tejinder Kaur and N.K. Neb. *Perspectives on Diaspora Indian Fiction in English.* Jalandhar: Nirman Pub., 2005.

Singh, Manjeet Inder. *Contemporary Diasporic Literature: Writing History*, Culture, Self. New Delhi: Pencraft International, 2007.

6

The Matrix and Dynamics of Female Oppression

Supriya Shukla

Confounded at the ongoing trend among women writers of perpetually exposing the vulnerability of their female characters Lisa Lau Ee Jia States:

> Curiously, majority of South Asian women writers appear to consistently posit their protagonists and female characters as victims, not so much as a result of class, caste, or even circumstances, and primarily and simply because they are women. This emphasis on the victimhood of South Asian women has been so prominent that it has almost become a characteristic of the genre.[1]

Two novels, Shauna Singh Baldwin's *What the Body Remembers* (1999) and Manju Kapur's *Difficult Daughters* (1998) have been selected for analyzing the causes for and implications of this particular issue. Both the novels, one featuring a protagonist who confirms and the other, a protagonist who rebels emphasize on the victimization of women. Both submission and defiance relegate women to the role of victims. The tradition-bound male-dominated Indian social matrix is accountable for this kind of victimization. Women have been and still continue to be discriminated in lieu of their sex. Indian women have to bear the brunt of living and struggling under patriarchal pressure. The family and society become intimidating prescriptive factors in life and are largely responsible for the rigid standards of morality imposed upon the Indian woman, who, instead of emerging as a self-determining individual is cursed with playing a subordinate role in every field of life. It is this oppression reflected in the writings of South Asian women writers which shows that womanhood in India can be equated with victimhood.

Shauna Singh Baldwin, as a Canadian born Indian Sikh has a complex cultural identity—an author who is a computer whiz, with a master's degree in business educated in India and is now living in Milwaukee, Wisconsin. She moved to the United States since it was forced on her when Canadian universities refused to acknowledge her Indian degree. Thus claiming three nationalities, fluent in English, Urdu, French and Punjabi, and her marriage with an Irish-American have given her a richly-informed world view that she weaves into her books. Though a second generation Canadian, Baldwin grew up in India and spent her formative years in New Delhi. A thirst for a deeper understanding of Indian history culminated in the making of her first novel *What the Body Remembers* and established her as an internationally acclaimed author. The novel won the 2000 Commonwealth Prize for Best Book in the Canadian Caribbean region and has been translated into fourteen languages.

What the Body Remembers, with the brutal drama of the 1947 partition as its backdrop probes into the status and psyche of women. The story is about two women married to the same man and the evolving relationship between the three. It focuses on the two women—Satya and Roop and their husband Sardarji, exhibiting all human emotions of love and hate, pride and jealousy, fertility and infertility and above all the sufferings of the two women.

The interesting thing is that the oppressor and the oppressed, both are women. The elder woman, Satya married to Sardarji has been unable to give an heir to the family. Though still beautiful at the age of 42 she is childless and thus urges Sardarji, her well-bred husband to marry a young girl of sixteen, twenty-five years younger to him. Roop belongs to a poor Sikh family and feels extremely fortunate to be wedded to

Sardarji even as his second wife. In course of time she gives birth to a daughter and then two sons. Though Sardarji is proud to have fathered two sons he is more attached to Satya and his sons. Roop, for him, is only fertile land for sowing seeds. However, Satya is plagued by intense jealousy and inflicts cruelties on Roop who desperately tries to please. This has a debilitating effect on Roop so much so that she stops eating, falls sick and goes back to her native place. Sardarji realizes his mistake and brings her back to Rawalpindi but has to agree to the condition laid down by Roop's father and brother that Roop should be separated from Satya and be allowed to live with her children who have been living under the guardianship of Satya till now. This brings about a partition in his own family at a time when India and Pakistan are partitioned. The familial as well as the national tragedy runs parallel in the novel. Thus the elder woman, Satya becomes the oppressor and the younger, Roop is the oppressed. However, tables are turned when Roop retaliates in her own way by going back to her father's place and the ensuing circumstances which lead to the separation of Satya from Sardarji.

The mental agony accompanied by this psychological upheaval shatters the Sardarji. The novelist finely portrays the separation of Sardarji from his beloved wife, Satya, making adjustments with Roop on one hand, and the changing political situation on the other hand. Though, he lives with Roop he is constantly reminded of Satya who has occupied his body and soul. It is now Satya who is victimized. She meets with a tragic death finally. However, when she is grappling with tuberculosis and is in the final stages of the fatal disease, she receives respect and honour from her husband which is gratifying for her. Her efforts to reign supremely in her husband's heart do get fulfilment. Sardarji is torn between two loyalties and finds it difficult to maintain harmony in the family. Baldwin probes into the psyche of her main characters through her well-knit plot portraying the intense tragedy at the familial and the political level.

> *What the Body Remembers* is a powerful combination of historical and domestic drama, making a promising debut for Shauna Singh Baldwin.[2]

Baldwin grapples with the age-old issue of woman as being the oppressor as well as the oppressed. But the question is whether the woman as oppressor is a social 'construct' or an essential individual. Linda Alcoff argues,

> We are constructs—that is our experience of our very subjectivity is a construct mediated by and/or grounded in a social discourse beyond (way beyond) individual control.[3]

In case of Satya the oppressor's identity is a 'construct' in a sense that she has to impose her superiority in order to maintain her identity. Her subjective position is socially accepted. In the community she gets more respect than Sardarji. Satya's decision to raise Roop's children is seen by the Sikh community as justified though her own female heart craves for a child.

Roop, on the other hand, is the perfect foil—a woman who is ornamental. She marries Sardarji to escape from the world of poverty and grief. She becomes not only a vessel for Sardarji's seeds but also an object on whom Sardarji may assert his superior masculinity which he cannot do with Satya. Thus Roop finds herself in a world dominated by both patriarchy and feudalism. However, slowly Roop gains hold. She protests for an honourable status in the household. Her age, beauty and capacity to bear children become the reins which guide and control Sardarji. As she starts getting a stronger hold on him, there begins her struggle for a greater self-expression. But the complete self-expression manifests itself only after Satya's death. Satya's spirit bold, proud and capable—imbues Roop with her courage on a more cynical clear-eyed view of her own situation and life, specially during her perilous journey with her children from Lahore, Pakistan to Delhi, India in search of safety.

Baldwin explains,

> *What the Body Remembers* is a very feminist book if you define feminism as the radical notion that a woman

> is a person—it depends on how accustomed you are to women having rights as people, including the right to own their own body. It comments on woman to woman power relations, surrogate motherhood and the two strains of feminism, strident and persuasive, that we have in operation today. Nevertheless, the women in this novel are also trapped in their gender, religion, time and cultures too—as we all are in every time and culture, there is nothing new in the universe.[4]

Manju Kapur's maiden venture, *Difficult Daughters* lucidly focuses on the fundamental issue of woman oppression in a male-dominated society. The novel gives a threadbare analysis of modern dynamics of man-woman relationship, particularly in the context of the Indian, social background. The novel primarily deals with the intellectual and emotional dilemma faced by an educated daughter of a conservative joint family of India. It gives a realistic portrayal of women of three successive generations with Virmati, the difficult daughter holding centre-stage. A thorough study of the novel obviously exhibits the treatment of three separate composite sets of Indian women. All the three sets categorically centre around the very idea and spirit of marriage in the Indian context. The first set consists of women characters like Lajwanti, Kasturi, Kishori Devi, Harish's mother and his first wife, Ganga. Their marriages date back to the pre-independence era and therefore they seem to behave in a similar manner. Their minds are attuned to the institution of marriage as the be-all and end-all in life. They naturally glorify marriage as for them it is the moral aspect that counts. The novelist likewise tries to show this approach through Ganga's mind-set:

> Her husband continued to be Ganga's public statement of selfhood. Her bindi and her bangles, her toerings and her mangalsutra, all managed to suggest he was still her god.[5]

When the psyche is moulded by firmly entrenched social beliefs and shaped by antiquated preconceived concepts, one can never think freely and absolve oneself of the fetters of socially accepted norms. Women at a relatively advanced stage of life, labouring under the various compulsions, enjoy less social and psychological freedom, than men and are forced to live their lives in the shadow, first, of parental dominance, and then of patriarchal oppression. Thus Manju Kapur's first set of women characters face this sort of male dominance in their lives.

The remaining two sets of women, comprising the second and third generation of the women folk of that family, vividly visualize the social scenario round about the independence of India and onwards. Virmati, her cousin Shakuntala and her hostel room-mate, Swarnalata constitute the second set.

The position of a woman in the community is socially construed and is apt to change with the times. Freedom and censure have both been integral parts of a woman's life and women who have refused to buckle under patriarchal pressure have very often succeeded in changing their own lives and those of others dependent on them. However, such bold women have had to face stiff opposition and unaccountable humiliation to lead a life of their own choice. One such woman is Virmati who has been placed in a private, domestic world where emotions and feelings are her bridge to experience but with education bringing enlightenment and empowerment she is equipped to challenge confidently the traditional framework of knowledge and to steer her way through familial and social oppression and discrimination to secure her own place in society and to realise her own worth. Virmati strives to overcome the prescriptive norms of her family and society by breaking free from the shackles of tradition, by pursuing higher education and marrying the man of her choice. This journey is ardous and also heart-breaking for her at times but she is undeterred by the hazards and follows her own path.

The third set includes Chhoti and Ida, the narrator who is a divorce and a childless woman. The gamut of the story revolves around Ida, the third-generation protagonist, Virmati her mother and Kasturi, her grandmother who finally comes to terms with her difficult daughter, Virmati. Ida wittingly remarks that she would not like to be a replica of her mother as her mother had not been like her grandmother. Ida, probably, in saying so, is conscious of her own lapse in having failed to understand her mother, to connect with her and to empathize with her in the traumatic sequence of events in her life. This kind of love-hate relationship between mother and daughter invariably emerges as a consequence of the mother's efforts to introduce checks and restraints in the unbridled activities of the daughter. Conscious of the autobiographical resonance of the mother-daughter relationship Manju Kapur remarks,

> Conflict between daughter and mother is inevitable and I suppose I was a difficult daughter. The conflict carries on through generations because mothers want their daughters to be safe. We want them to make the right choices—right in the sense that they are socially acceptable. My mother wanted me to be happily married, I want my daughters to have good jobs.[6]

Ida gathers information about her mother's past when she visits Amritsar and meets her kith and kin. The narrative is developed in a unique manner by co-existing the past and the present. As the story goes Virmati, the eldest of ten siblings lives in a conservative joint family in Amritsar. She is bogged down by the charge she is given of looking after her siblings and her mother during her successive pregnancies. She is soon considered to be eligible for marriage and is engaged to Indrajeet. However, she is inspired by her cousin, Shakuntala, an M.Sc. in Chemistry, to experience freedom and lead a life of her own so that she can shoulder other responsibilities rather than those of a husband and children. Shakuntala is a woman of a liberal, radical and revolutionary mind-set who leaves home and moves to Lahore to participate in the Freedom Struggle. Shakuntala's maverick lifestyle generate a new urge and craving in Virmati to free herself from the bondage of patriarchy that denies her the freedom of choice.

This is the focal point where the novel and the protagonist's life takes a dynamic turn. Her marriage to Indrajeet is postponed due to a death in his family and Virmati luckily convinces her mother who reluctantly allows her to study further. She enters A.S. College and it is here that she notices and is noticed by the Oxford returned Professor, Harish Chandra, who is also her neighbour. Then begins Virmati's cataclysmic journey swayed by passion for the already married man. Virmati rejects the pre-arranged marriage, attempts suicide and is confined to the four walls of a storehouse when her family learn of her affair. Realizing the hopelessness of illicit love she leaves for Lahore to pursue advanced studies. Defying patriarchal constraints she asserts herself to attain self-reliance through education. Though she shuns the professor's company as he is unable to deal with the domestic tangle, yet she eventually does succumb to his implorations to grant him clandestine meetings and consequently soon finds herself pregnant. A sense of guilt at this loss of virginity and an unwed pregnancy starts gnawing at her mind. Though she does wish to indulge in "meaningful activities" like her room-mate Swarnlata, she is dissuaded to do so by the Professor. She gets the child secretly aborted but her resoluteness and tenacity wane. As far as their marriage, the professor keeps deferring it. Later when he does marry her at a friend's insistence, Virmati is not given the status due to her. In her effort to please him, she is reduced almost to a non-entity. Thus the rebel in Virmati seems to have lost confidence. She now feels emotionally, intellectually and physically shattered for she is dependent on the professor. She is suffering from what Chaman Nahal calls "the dependence syndrome"[7] which is the need to fall back on someone in times of crises.

It is absurd that though Virmati defies age-old traditions, she tried to persuade her daughter Ida to conform to the values upheld by the family. She fails to do so as Ida develops into an intractable woman, never making an effort to understand her mother. So the predicament of the three women of three generations Kasturi, Virmati and Ida—is not a private one but a synthesis of the complex social structure, family attitudes and the man-woman relationship in each one's life.

The portrayal of women in Indian English fiction does not focus on depicting the image of a complete and perfect woman. Women are simply meant to suffer upto martyrdom. The austere, male-dominated society does not let her grow into a resolute independent individual.

Manju Kapur's *Difficult Daughters* gives a vital message to Indian women which explains the new dynamics visible in the Indian social framework. She seems to suggest that mere rejection of societal norms is not enough. A woman must have the tenacity of purpose to fulfil her own aims and ambitions. She must be self-reliant and rational and must continue to have faith in herself despite all odds she has to encounter. The untenable, the unjust and the unethical should always be challenged and demolished by her. She should not be steered through life by men but by her own perceptions and insight. As Kalpana R.J. affirms,

> Women must be given freedom within their chosen life patterns and freedom in choosing alternative life patterns.[8]

To achieve this women need to be well-educated, to be daring to protest and put up a brave fight against all kinds of man-made affliction created by the male-dominated society. Only then can they be exonerated from the claustrophobic detention of misery. Perseverance, dogged determination and strength of will have brought about visible changes in society for the educated and enlightened woman. However, women must continue to strive and forge ahead to acquire a respectable status for as Virginia Woolf puts it,

> No thing follows a regular course. The paths wind between bogs and precipices, the trees roar and rock and fall into ruin.[9]

Thus both Shauna Singh Baldwin and Manju Kapur inadvertently portray the victimization of women through their novels. *What the Body Remembers* and *Difficult Daughters* have in common the 1947 partition of the subcontinent as their main theme. Yet both the novelists reflect on the status of women in society. Though Baldwin attempts to give a Sikh perception of the partition yet the physical vivisection of the subcontinent is not emphasized by her. What she lays stress on is the psychological upheaval in the lives of her characters. She focuses her attention more on the stories of Sardarji, Satya and

Roop and their mental conflicts. Roop submits to societal, parental and patriarchal pressures and yet suffers. Despite begetting heirs for the family she suffers at the hands of Satya. She is denied the fundamental right of the guardianship of her own children. She does not get the position that she should in the family. Thus submission and passive conformity to familial and social norms does not spare the Indian woman from oppression. Satya, Sardarji's first wife though has an upper hand and a respectable status in her family. However, Satya too has to bear her share of agony. She suffers from emotional insecurity as she is childless and unable to give an heir to the family. Her conflict and trauma due to her physical inability and her husband's desire of a male heir drives her to urge her husband to marry Roop. With the second marriage and the fulfillment of Sardarji's dreams of begetting an heir Satya struggles to maintain her status in the family. She exercises her power and motivates her husband to give her sole custody of the children even though her health is deteriorating. To maintain the statues quo she tries to dominate Roop as she feels threatened of being neglected due to the changed circumstances within the family. The oppressed and the oppressor both are sufferers, and victims of social oppression.

Manju Kapur's chief protagonist in *Difficult Daughters* may be termed as a rebel as she defies familial traditions and charts an independent course of life. However, defiance spells doom for her. Virmati belongs to a conservative Punjabi family and as the eldest daughter tries to fulfil her filial duties. Her share of problems arises when she falls in love with a married professor, something that is considered highly immoral and unacceptable in society. Further, inspired by her cousin Shakuntala she takes another bold step of moving to Lahore for higher education. The professor's insistence of secret meetings lands her into further trouble as she finds herself with his child. Virmati undergoes the trials and tribulations of a love that has little hope of social acceptance. She goes through the trauma of aborting the unwanted pregnancy. Virmati's humble and heroic suffering in order to secure her love and marriage with the already married professor, the social opprobrium that she has to suffer, even after she is married to the professor, at the hands of his mother and first wife, the social ostracism that she faces so much so that she is not allowed to visit her parent's house even for the funeral of her own father symbolizes her assertiveness to carve a niche for herself. Here her suffering is mainly due to the inconsiderate attitude of her lover as Suman Bala and Subhash Chandra explain:

> But her acceptance of the treatment meted out to her by her lover, the professor, totally belies these expectations. The professor's pursuit of Virmati even after she has been sent to Lahore as part of a punishment to study in Women's College, his renewing sexual relations with her with full ardour, but his reluctance and constant postponing of the marriage inspite of her frequent entreaties to do so, are instances of the gratifications of the male desire. Male ego-centricism blinds men to the situation of women, who may be placed in agonizing circumstances on account of their relationship with men.[10]

In Virmati we find a woman caught in the conflict between the passions of the flesh and a yearning to be a part of the political and intellectual movements of the day. Her room-mate Swarnalata who is actively involved in the struggle for independence infuses in her the desire to participate in political activities so much so that she starts feeling that she should not waste her life in useless love and a doubtful marriage and concentrate on joining others to fight a common enemy. However, as luck would have it she gets married to the professor, is harassed perpetually by his family and finally restores her dignity and self respect by going back to Lahore for a postgraduate course in philosophy. Ida is conceived and she goes through her pregnancy successfully. Finally she is also forgiven by her mother, Kasturi and she moves to her mother's house to feed scores of people who, on fleeing from Pakistan, pass through Amritsar.

Successfully recreating India's painful passage into a new nation, Manju Kapur weaves with this political birth Virmati's story of rebellion and her quest for independence. The novel touches myriad issues like revolt against deep-rooted family tradition, the search for selfhood, women's rights, marriage and the battle for independence at both fronts—personal and national. After the turbulent events of 1947 Virmati and the professor find some peace. Ida too in reliving those years is ready to begin life afresh. Along with suffering are mingled hope and its renewal.

Both the novels analysed clearly indicate that social life in India swarms with problems—"vagaries and varieties"[11] as Iyengar refers to them. These social problems are more likely to plague the female section of society. A woman needs to extricate herself from her cumbrous circumstances and emerge from the psychic bondage she may find herself in. Women writers are endeavouring to tell the world that it is not gender equality as a prerequisite for an ideal marriage that they are advocating for a woman but a certain freedom within the community of men and women that will fulfil them. Thus they want their female protagonists "to explore their own potential or to live on their own terms regardless of the consequences that such a rebellion may have on their lives."[12]

This search for identity and space is what women novelists are striving to express and achieve for their own species.

It is heartening to note that some positive changes in society is becoming apparent slowly and steadily. Shiv K. Kumar identifies this as

> a gradual shift in values that has been taking place in this subcontinent during the past two decades or so.[13]

The age-old debate of why women suffer probably has a universal conclusion that brings into focus the concepts and bias attached to gender which are again man-made. The fault lies with their gender, not with them. Simon de Beauvoir rightly observes:

> One is not born, but rather becomes a woman. It is civilization as a whole that produces this creature—which is described as feminine.[14]

However, the modern dynamics of man-woman relationship particularly in the Indian social background has deflected from the general to the individual's quest for selfhood. Indian women writers now are reflecting the graph of social changes in India through their female protagonists in their novels. The Indian society, so bogged down by tradition, could not remain impervious to the new forces that had started making their impact felt and the new awakenings that had started making inroads into the minds of people. Creative women writers like Anita Desai, Nayantara Sahgal, Shashi Deshpande, Bharati Mukherjee, Kamala Markandaya, Manju Kapur have tried to re-define woman's status in society.

The emancipation of the Indian woman and the Indian English novel has for some time been advancing together. Women, "the disqualified half of the human race"[15] as John Stuart Mill calls them are now straddling the wall between tradition and modernity. Indian novelists, specially women writers are being vocal about the modern Indian woman striving for compatibility between self-worth and independence, and a deep-rooted commitment to her various relationships, primarily that of a wife. Even if she suffers she is not weak as Bhagat Nayak puts it,

> ...in a male dominated society where laws for women are made by men in its social matrix, a husband stands as a sheltering tree under which a woman proves her strength through her suffering.[16]

Sufferings evince her real strength. This power politics which divides the male and female into the oppressor and the oppressed is still all pervasive and needs to be mitigated.

In order to get over this complex, a re-orientation of the mental attitudes of men and women is absolutely essential and there needs to be a constant reviewing of masculine and feminine approaches to all aspects of life.

To sum up the context of the two novels taken up for study—Shauna Singh Baldwin's *What the Body Remembers* and Manju Kapur's *Difficult Daughters*—the former illustrates the social matrix and milieu whereas the latter definitely heralds the dynamics of a visible change towards a progressive society.

NOTES

1. Lisa Lau Ee Jua, "Equating Womanhood with Victimhood: the positionality of women protagonists in the contemporary writings of South Asian women", *Women's Studies International Forum,* Vol. 26, Issue 4, July-August 2003.
2. Sheila Bright, Editorial Reviews, Amazon.com
3. Linda Alcoff, "Cultural Feminism versus Post Structuralism: The Identity in Feminist Theory" in *Feminism and Philosophy*, ed. Nancy Tauna and Rose Marie Teng (London: Westview Press Inc., 1995), p. 40.
4. http://randomhouse.com
5. Manju Kapur, *Difficult Daughters* (New Delhi: Penguin India, 1998), p. 257.
6. Cited in Suman Bala and Subhash Chandra, "Manju Kapur's Difficult Daughters: An absorbing tale of fact and fiction", *Fifty Years Of Indian Writing* (New Delhi: IAES, 1999), p. 107.
7. Chaman Nahal, "Feminism in English Fiction: Forms and Variations", *Feminism and Recent Fiction in English,* ed. Sushila Singh (New Delhi, Prestige, 1991), p. 17.
8. Kalpana, R.J., *Feminism and Family* (New Delhi: Prestige Books, 2005), p. 25.
9. Virginia Woolf, Harriette Wilson, *Collected Essays*, ed. Leonard Woolf (London: Hogarth Press, 1966), VI, III, p. 227.
10. Suman Bala and Subhash Chandra, "Manju Kapur's Difficult Daughters: An absorbing tale of fact and fiction", *Fifty Years of Indian Writing*, New Delhi: IAES, 1999.
11. K.R.S. Iyengar, *Indian Writing in English* (Bombay: Asia Publishing House, 1973, 2nd Edition), p. 327.
12. Anita Ghosh, "Women on Top: A study of Feministic Consciousness in Modern Indian Women Novelists," *New Lights on Indian Women Novelists in English* (Part II) ed. Amar Nath Prasad (New Delhi: Sarup and Sons, 2004), pp. 250-51.
13. Shiv K. Kumar, "Tradition and Change in the Novels of Kamala Markandaya", *Osmania Journal of English Studies*, 7/1 (1969), p. 1.

14. Simone de Beauvoir, *The Second Sex*, trans and ed. H.M. Parshley, 1953 (Harmondsworth: Penguin, Rpt. 1983), p. 295.
15. John Stuart Mill, *The Subjection of Women* (1869) (Essay) (Lucknow: Gurukul Publication, Rpt. 2000), p. 99.
16. Bhagbat Nayak, "Manju Kapur's Difficult Daughters: A Feminist Reading", *Indian Journal of English Studies*, Vol. XXXVIII, p. 103.

7

Vastu, Neta and *Rasa* in Indian Poetics and the Concepts of Greek Drama

Vachaspati Dwivedi

In the wake of post-colonial theory and its negative/positive repercussions on the already existing theories, one often finds himself in a dilemma in selecting parameters for the evaluation/ appreciation of literature. Edward Said's *Orientalism* (1978), the theory's founding work, deals with "Orientalism" and the dilemmas of developing a national identity after the days of colonial rule and the various ways in which writers from colonized countries attempt to articulate the cultural identities and reclaim it as a "cultural contestant" (Mohanty, 2007: 20). Bill Ashcroft's essay "The Empire Writes Back" observes it as a resistance by the colonized to the colonizer and describes these indigenous writings as a response to the colonized legacy by writing back to the centre (Ascroft, *et at.*, 1989). Viewed in this paradigm, the last decade of Indian English criticism has been liberating enough in the sense that it has extended its canvas to traditional poetics, both Sanskrit and Tamil, by applying their concepts to modern texts and genres (Girish Karnad, Krishna Rayan, Kapil Kapoor) and it is working for the evolution of a nativist paradigm which tries to postulate an authentic historiography of the literature of the regional languages (G.N. Devi, Meenakshi Mukherjee, Harish Trivedi) and the rejection of the western stereotypes. Their work approves a cross examination of the Western and Indian concepts for criticism as it cannot be done by evaluating them in isolation. As Krishna Rayan opines, "such cross examination only enhances the accuracy of our perception (...). Even if the Sanskrit poetic were to insulate itself form all that is western and modern, it would still have to respond to the extensive and vigorous perception and experiment in literary practice within the Indian system, much of which is inspired by Western and modernist writing and theory" (1994: 16). It is in communion with elemental human nature as Chari writes, "the essential human experience that literature communicates is not historically or culturally conditioned but appeals to what is most basic and elemental in human nature" (1990: 247). The present paper intends to analyse the concepts of *Vastu*, *Neta* and *Rasa* proposed by ancient Sanskrit scholars like Anandvardhana, Abhinavagupta, Bharata, Mammata, Dhananjaya and others in order to evaluate its relevance for the growth of a native Indian literary discourse in English.

'Poetry' in Sanskrit poetics is divided in two kinds—*Dristya* 'what is capable of being seen or exhibited' and *Sravya* 'what can only be heard or sung'. Drama falls in the first category. It is called *Rupaka*, a term given for all dramatic compositions encompassing a secondary class *Uparupaka* as well. *Rupaka* has *Rasa* (sentiments) as its base. Dhananjaya divides *Rupaka* in ten classes:

> *Awasthanu kritirnatyam rupamdrisyatyochyate*
>
> *Rupakam tatsamaropat dashdhaiwa rasasrayam.*
>
> (*Natya* is imitation of different situations in (the scenes presented by) life. *Natya* is also called *Rupa* in as much as it has *dristya* or the capability of being seen, its subject-matter is represented by actors assuming particular characters. It is based on *Rasa* and is of ten types). (Dhananjaya, 1988: 4)
>
> *Natakam saprakarnam bhanah prahasanam dimah*
>
> *Vyayogsamvakaro veethyankehamriga iti.*
>
> (These types are *nataka, prakarana, bhanah, prahasana, dima, vyayoga, samvakaro, veethi, ankah and ihamriga.*) (*Ibid.*, 5)

Rupaka has three main constituents as the life blood of every dramatic piece—*vastu* (plot), *neta* (hero) and *rasa* (sentiment). *Vastu* has been classified in two kinds, *adhikarik* (principal) and *prasangik* (accessory). *Adhikarik* is related to the chief protagonist or characters of the main plot of *rupaka*. The *prasangik* is related to what happens other than the main topic and it encompasses the characters other than the hero and the heroine. *Vastu* has five essential *arthaprakaris* (requisites) for its development. These are *bija* (the seed), *bindu* (the drop), *pataka* (the banner), *prakari* (the episode) and *karya* (the final issue). *Bija* is the circumstance leading to the ultimate result briefly stated which as the plot takes its shape, gives multifarious results as the seed of the plot. *Bindu* joins any break of sequence in the plot if caused by the addition of an incident. *Pataka* is an episode which either illustrated, advances or stops the progress of plot in order to add interest in it. *Prakari* is an episode of limited duration having minor importance. The principal characters do not have any part in it. *Karya* is the main object of the plot after whose attainment the drama ends. These *arthaprakaris* in perfect combination with *awasthas* (stages of development) result in *samdhis* (junctures). *Awasthas* (stages) are five in number—*aarambha* (beginning), *yatna* (effort), *praptyasha* (prospect of success), *niyatapti* (attainment after crossing obstacles) and *falagam* (the result of getting the desired aim).

> *Awastha panchakaryasya prasabhdhasya falarthibhi*
> *Arambha yatna praptyasha niyatapti falagamah.*
> (Kaviraja, 1922: 298)

Samdhis connect these *awasthas* and *arthaprakatris*. These are *mukha* (the opening), *pratimukha* (the means to the chief end), *garbha* (attainment or non-attainment of the end), *awamarsha* (*peripeteia*) and *nirrahana* (catastrophe):

> *Mukham pratimukham garbho vimarsha upasamhritih*
> *Iti panchasya bhedah syuh kramalakshanyuchyate.*
> (*Ibid.*, 299)

Mukhasamdhi is the combination of the *bija* and *aarambha* in which the *bija* is sown with all its *rasas*. The *pratimukha* has *yatna* (means) which leads the hero to the chief end, implied by the *bija* in the *mukha* which sprouts up there. In the *garbha* there is attainment and non-attainment of the desired end implying a further sprouting up of the original *bija*. The *awamarshasamdhi* is that in which the seed attains a more luxuriant growth being accompanied by *niyatapti* of the end put whose final result is postponed further off. The *nirranana* or consummation is the harmonious combination of all the aforesaid parts in the final catastrophe.

Here it is observed that the concept of *neta* (hero) is at total variance with the Aristotelian concept of hero because of the fact that there are no tragedies in Sanskrit literature. In the Indian concept the hero should be modest, decorous, comely, munificent, civil, of sweet address and eloquent in his character. Above all he must belong to a noble family. *Neta* is of four kinds—*dhirodatta, dhiralalita, dhirashanta* and *dhirodhhatta*. *Dhiralalita* is the hero who is graceful and firm as described:

Nischinto madhuranisham kalaparo dhiralalita syat.

(*Ibid.*, 98)

Each of these heroes may be one or other of these types. He may be *dakshina* or gallant who is equally devoted to many women, though principally attached to one. The *shantha* hero is that who being attached to one lady, acts in a way unpleasant to her, or he may be *dhrista* or bold who openly makes his professions to another, and not ashamed even when reproached, or lastly he may be *anukul* or favourable who is devoted to one heroine only. Among the assistants of the hero is *Peethamard* who acts as hero of the *pataka* or episode, clever in discourse, devoted to his master and a little inferior to him in his qualities. Next is *Vidushaka*, his constant companion who indulges in repartees of wit, and whose business is to help his friend in his love—intrigues and thus assisting in the general *denouement* of the play.

Bhava or 'feeling' is the complete perversion of the heart by any emotion, whether of pleasure or pain, arising from the object under sight; *Vibhava* or an excitant (determinant) is that which being perceived nourishes the main sentiment. It is divided in (1) *Alambana*, which is the person or thing with reference to whom or which a sentiment arises, such as the hero or the heroine, and (2) *Uddipana*, or what excites or enhances the sentiment, such as the moon, the beauties of the vernal season, the beauty of the characters or decorations in the case of *Sringara*. *Anubhava*, or the consequent is the outward manifestation of the internal feeling through the eyes or face. The *Sattvika* or natural bhavas are subdivisions of *Anubhava*. The *Vyabhicharis* or the moods are those bhavas that are not strictly confined to any *Rasa*, but they appear and disappear and serve as feeders to the prevailing sentiment and strengthen it in different ways. *Sthayibhavas* or the permanent sentiment of a composition assimilates all into one form as "the ocean melting all salt into water—which not being interrupted by any sentiment contrary or akin to its nature occurring at intervals, converts all of them into its own nature" (*Ibid.*, 217).

Abhinavagupta mentions 'nine heads' under which *Rasa* can be studied. These nine are *sthayins* (permanent emotions). These are mutually elusive and lay inert in the hearts of the people. When a stimulus activates them, they sprung out as corresponding *rasas*. A poet conveys these or any one of these emotions through his poem by using objective correlatives like images, situations or suggestions. When a reader is affected with these, the corresponding *sthayin* within him is evoked raising it to the level of *rasa* in him. These *sthayins* are *Rati* (the sexual emotion), *Hasa* (laughter), *Shoka* (grief/distress), *Krodha* (anger), *Utsaha* (masterfulness), *Bhaya* (fear), *Jugupsa* (disgust), *Vismaya* (wonder) and *Sama* (subsidence) (Bhratmuni, 1971: 608) on which are based respectively the sentiments of *Shringara* (the erotic), *Hasya* (the comic), *Karuna* (the pathetic), *Roudra* (the furious), *Veera* (the heroic), *Bhayanaka* (the terrible), *Veebhatsa* (the loathsome), *Adbhuta* (the marvellous) and *Shanta* (the serene). Out of these nine, *Shringara* and *Hasya*, *Veera* and *Adbhuta*, *Veebhatsa* and *Bhayanaka* and *Roudra* and *Karuna* are akin to each other as they proceed from the same condition of mind. *Rati* (erotic) is mainly the prevailing sentiment in most Sanskrit plays and it is divided into *Vipralambha* (love-in-separation) and *Sambhoga* (love-in-union). Dhananjaya divides *Vipralambha* in two kinds.

Ayoga, the non-consummation of marriage, and *Viprayoga*, the separation of the lovers deep in love after marriage. *Sambhoga* is when the two lovers are in enjoyment of each other or kissing each other. The chief end for a work of art is the emergence of rasa, the sap or juice as the primary element of literature facilitating rasaswadana (relishing) and understanding the work of art. Rasa is the aesthetic feeling aroused in the readers due to the miraculous effect of sound and meaning. According to De, "the perception of suggested rasa (...) involves a process, but from its quickness the process is not perceived, like the process (...) of the apparently simultaneous piercing or a hundred lotus-leaves placed upon one another" (1976: 162). It leaves the mind of the reader in a state of joy and fulfilment not to be found in the cathartic effect of Aristotle. There is no equivalent to rasa in Western aesthetics. It may be, to some extent, compared to Longines' "Sublime" but there lies a lot of difference. The epic *Ramayana* explicates *Karuna rasa* whereas the Mahabharata is an assimilation of *Veera, Raudra, Karuna, Veebhatsa* and *Bhayanaka* etc. The dominant rasa in *Gitanjali* is *bhakti* or 'love' for God. The ardent devotion that the poet feels for Him pervades the whole *Gitanjali* and causes the dominant *bhakti rasa*. Similarly other works explicate other *rasas*.

Every dramatic piece opens with a prelude which is introduced through *Nandipath* (recitation of Prelude). *Nandi* suggests the gist of whole plot to the audience. The *Sutradhara* may retire after *Nandipath* by giving place to *Sthapaka* on the stage. The Prelude either begins with a short introduction to the poet's literary achievements or his genealogy etc. after which the *Sutradhara* or the *Sthapaka* introduce the subject in the form of *Bija*. They try to please the audience by melodious songs describing some sweet season like spring. After the Prelude the drama begins in the way as stated in the previous pages. It is divided into five to ten acts and scenes that are well shaped to give the impression of a complete whole.

The *Neta* (hero) should be of *Dhirodatta* class who should cause the sentiment of *Shringara*, *Veera* or *Karuna*. The acts must not be tiresome because of their length and must be full of *Rasa*. The incidents like journeys, murders or wars must not be shown on stage, rather they should be indicated. The death of the hero is never to be exhibited on stage in Sanskrit Poetics and this states the reason for the total absence of tragedies in ancient India. The play ends as it begins with a *Bharatvakya* (a benediction or prayer) which is repeated by the chief protagonist not as a dramatic character but as a member of the dramatic party and contains their wishes for general prosperity and happiness. The language is classical Sanskrit for the main characters whereas the minor characters may speak in different Prakrit dialects.

Compared to the Indian dramas the Greek dramas stand poles apart. Indian plays never reach a calamitous conclusion that can be sufficient to result in tragedy. They never leave any painful impression upon the audience whereas the structure of Greek drama has an essential feature of conflict in it. The theme of tragedy is dark and serious whereas the comedies are light and happy and they mostly end in marriages. Similar to the five *arthaprakaris* of *Vastu* for its development in Indian drama, Greek tragedy has five stages—exposition, complication, climax, denouement (falling action) and a catastrophe (solution) which decides the fate of its characters. The exposition explains the precondition from which the action springs out. Complication progresses the action to its climax. Climax denotes the stage when it takes a better or worse turn, denouement is the falling action which unfolds the complication resulting in either a solution (in comedy) or catastrophe (in tragedy). Taking a cue form Seneca, the Greek playwright, the Elizabethan drama was divided into five acts each related to the five stages working through different scenes. The aim of both the genres is to give pleasure like the Sanskrit drama resulting by its *rasas* as tragedy inspires us with pity and fear resulting in purgation whereas comedy aims at evoking laughter in the audience. The hero of a tragedy is of noble society or a man of high birth, the interest of comedy being people of much less importance.

The Encyclopedia Britannica defines tragedy as "drama of a serious and dignified character that typically describes the development of a conflict between the protagonist and a superior force (such as destiny, circumstance, or society) and reaches a sorrowful or disastrous conclusion" (2006, 10, p. 7). Comedy on the other hand is a "genre of dramatic literature that deals with the light and amusing or with the serious and produced in a light or satirical manner" (2006, 3, p. 16). Aristotle mentions six elements in a tragedy—plot, character, diction, thought, spectacle and song. Out of these, he stresses the importance of plot by saying, "...that the plot then, is the first principle, and, as it were, the soul of tragedy; character holds the second place" (Aristotle, 9). During the Renaissance the strong position of plot was suppressed by the emergence of strong individualistic characters of the Elizabethan age. The Shakespearean tragedies are all tragedies of character.

The plot must be a complete whole. It must show a beginning, middle and an end. Whatever is irrelevant must be eliminated and subordinated to the structure of the plot. All the incidents in it should be liked together in a probable or necessary sequence. Aristotle divides plot into two types—simple and complex. A simple plot is one without *peripeteia* and *anagnorisis*. *Peripeteia* is reversal of intention whereas *anagnorisis* means recognition or revelation of truth. A complex one has both, a fitting example being Sophocles' *Oedipus Rex*. Both the genres of Greek drama aim at giving pleasure. The Sanskrit drama aims at giving pleasure through the creation of different *rasas*, the Greek drama gives pleasure through the spectacle of human suffering and unhappy fate (in tragedy) and by showing "the common errors of life...in the most ridiculous and scornful sort that may be, so as it is impossible that any beholder can be content to be such a one" (Sidney, 1595, 1).

Tragedy affects a *catharsis* or purgation of emotions whereas comedy corrects the manners of the people. *Catharsis* refers to a cleansing or purgation of the unwanted emotions by means of the enactment of tragedy. It means a sensation, or literary effect that overcomes the audience upon finishing watching a tragedy. F.L. Lucas, on the other hand, maintains that *catharsis* cannot be defined as purification or cleansing, but only purgation. Aristotle used the term as a medical metaphor as "it is the human soul that is purged of its excessive passions" (1928: 24). Lucas negates the medical aspect of *catharsis* and defines it as an experience that brings pity and fear into their proper balance as "men are sometimes too much addicted to pity and fear, sometimes too little; tragedy brings them back to a virtuous and happy mean" (*Ibid.*, 23). Another important element of Greek drama is *hamartia* which is often explained as a mistake, fault or sin of the tragic hero. In *Nichomacean Ethics*, *hamartia* is explained by Aristotle as one of the three kinds of injuries man can commit to another man. It is an "injury committed in ignorance when the person affected is not what the agent supposed he was" (2002: 111). This implies that the protagonist commits a fatal mistake in complete ignorance. Othello's jealousy or Hamlet's irresolution, for example, can also be interpreted as moral flaws but their suffering and its traumatic effect is far out of proportion in comparison to the flaw. It is through *hamartia* that the audience experiences *catharsis*.

The other two features of classical drama are the three unities and the use of chorus. The theory of three unities has no parallel in Indian drama though there are suggestions for the organic unity of the plot. The element of chorus is replaced by the commentary of the *sutradhara* or the *nandipath*. The chorus consists of a body of actors who report what happened off the stage and make moral comments from time to time. The Classical tradition did not favour the representation of violent physical actions on the stage and it was reported by the chorus. The three unities—unity of time, unity of action and unity of place—were maintained though they limited the scope for the dramatists. Unity of time circumscribed the time of plot by limiting it to its time on stage. Unity of action sanctioned that the plot must not be a mixture of tragic and comic elements. This means that there must not be any comic relief as in the Elizabethan tragedies. Unity of place suggested that if the play limits itself to few hours, it needs to be stationed at one place. The romantic tragedies of Shakespeare do not comply to these unities or supreme importance to plot due to the reason that they represent the "new adventurous spirit of Elizabethan England, with its voyages of discovery and fascination" (*Encyclopedia Britannica*, 2009: 1). They take an important but imperfect person as their protagonist—Hamlet, Macbeth, King Lear, Othello, Dr. Faustus, Tamburlaine—all awe inspiring and over ambitious in their make. The presence of *Peethamard* and *Vidusaka* in Indian comedies finds its parallel in the characterization of fools in Shakespeare's comedies and history plays but they do not exist in Greek drama.

The present analysis is an attempt to underline the basic differences between the two critical schools as well as to stress upon the need of a new poetics with complete awareness of Indian poetics and its wise application. Keeping in view the new works of Indian drama (Girish Karnad) in English as well as in other Indian languages in the past decades, it becomes urgent and imperative as we can no way apply the alien concepts of English or Greek drama to them. This is because of the fact that the milieu, characters and themes are completely Indian. Indian poetics is profound enough to demand more study in the less explored areas like *Dhwani* and *Auchitya* to save ourselves from plenty of pseudo-critics who negate Indian English literature and Indian poetics.

REFERENCES

Aristotle. *Nichomachean Ethics*. Trans W.D. Ross, *Over 400 Works of Literature Database*. CD-ROM. Sidney: Eurekamultimedia, 2002.

———. *Poetics*. (tr.) S.H. Butcher. *Over 4000 Works of Literature Database*. Sidney: Eurekamultimedia, 2002.

Ascroft, Griffiths & Tiffin. *The Empire Writes Back: Theory and Practice in Post Colonial Literatures*. London: Rutledge, 1989.

Bharatmuni. *Natyashastram*. (ed.) Madhusudan Shastri. Varanasi: B.H.U. Press, 1971.

Britannica Ready Reference Encyclopedia. New Delhi: Encyclopedia Britannica (India) Pvt. Ltd., 2006.

Chari, V.K. *Sanskrit Criticism*. Honolulu: Hawaii University Press, 1990.

De, S.K. *Sanskrit Poetics*. Calcutta: Firma K.L., 1976.

Dhananjaya. *Dasrupakam.* (ed.) Bholasankar Vyas. Varanasi: Choukhambha Vidyabhavan, 1998.

Kaviraj, Viswanath. *Sahitya Darpana.* (ed. & tr.) Durga Prasad Dwivedi. Mumbai: Nirnay Sagar Press, 1922.

Lucas, F.L. *Tragedy in Relation to Aristotle's Poetics.* London: Hogarth, 1928.

Mongia, Padmini. (ed.) *Contemporary Postcolonial Theory.* New Delhi: O.U.P., 2007.

Rayan, Krishna. *Indian Literature.* No. 160, March-April, 1994, 14-17.

Sidney, Philip. *The Defence of Poesie.* As qtd. in "Comedy". Encyclopedia Britannica: *Ultimate Reference Suite.* Chicago: Encyclopedia Britannica, 2009.

"Tragedy". *Britannica Ready Reference Encyclopedia.* New Delhi: Encyclopedia Britannica (India) Pvt. Ltd., 2006.

"Tragedy". *Encyclopedia Britannica: Ultimate Reference Suite.* Chicago: Encyclopedia Britannica, 2009.

8

Voice of Protest in *Untouchable* and in *Choma's Drum*

R.P. Pradhan

Voices of protest are often heard in socio-political novels like *Untouchable* and *Choma's Drum*. Both the novels belong to 1930s of Indo-Anglian fiction and deal with the curse of untouchability in the caste-ridden Hindu society. Both of them cover a wide range of conservative Indian society from north to south in the pre-partition days. Mulk Raj Anand hailing from Peshawar in the North-West Frontier province of British India locates the action of *Untouchable* in a cantonment town in Punjab. On the other hand, Shivaram Karanth in *Choma's Drum* in Kannada literature portrays fundamental concerns of human existence through the life of a southern untouchable. Both the novelists reveal the agonies of their insulated heroes caused by the evils of social ostracism and social alienation.

The voice of protest in *Untouchable* is more vocal while in *Choma's Drum* it is silent but powerful in its artistic presentation. The charge of propaganda literature for some of the novels of Anand cannot be applicable in the case of *Untouchable* because "of all his novels *Untouchable* is the most compact and artistically satisfying."[1] The heroes of both the novels appear numb with despair because they are surrounded on all sides by socially superior men. However, their inner fury and external resentment break out in one way or the other from time to time. Bakha, the hero of *Untouchable* is more revolutionary and looks like a social rebel. He tells his father in a bitter manner: "They think we are mere dirt because we clean their dirt."[2]

Anand being the novelist of the underdog presents the ugly and seamy side of human life in this novel in a realistic manner. The mental condition and the spiritual anguish of his protagonist are revealed through the stream of consciousness technique. He describes a single day in the life of an eighteen year old sweeper boy named Bakha. He is the son of Lakha who is "the jemadar of all the sweepers in the town and the cantonment and officially in charge of the three rows of public latrines which lined the extreme end of the colony, by the brook-side."[3] Bakha gets up early in the morning and cleans them single-handed. After the fourth round of his work he feels thirsty and wants to drink tea but there is no water in the house for its preparation. An untouchable can get water only from the caste-well where he is not allowed to mount the platform. His sister Sohini stands eleven in the line for getting water. Pundit Kali Nath, one of the priests in the charge of the temple in the town favours her in giving water and calls her to clean the courtyard of his house at the temple. He tries to seduce her but as she cannot yield to his sexual desire, he propagates outside that he has been touched and hence polluted by a low-caste woman. Sohini told Bakha at the door of the courtyard "that man made suggestions to me, when I was cleaning the lavatory of his house there. And when I screamed, he came out shouting that he has been defiled."[4] The crowd on the temple believed "that he had suffered most grievously, and sympathised."[5] Sohini sobbed and Bakha asked her, "Tell me! Tell me! I will kill him if...."[6] Again he exclaimed, "Brahmin dog! I will go and kill him!"[7] His voice of protest becomes the voice of violence.

The dreams and aspirations of the hero in *Choma's Drum* are also crushed mercilessly in the same manner. The circumstances of both the untouchables, Bakha and Choma, appear to be different apparently but the fundamental issue is one and the same—how to maintain one's identity and existence in an orthodoxical society. In the case of Bakha it is a social and religious question, in the case of Choma it becomes an economic question. In both the cases, the hero is reduced to the level of a cog in the machine. The cog is the tooth on the wheel which makes the machine run. The untouchable sweeps and cleans the dirt and the excretion of society. The cog cannot question as to what the machine grinds. The untouchable cannot protest the social wrong and injustice done to him. However, both the novelists give voice to the aspirations and feelings of the underdog and the downtrodden. They make their heroes progressive and revoltive against the evils of cruel and inhuman society.

Choma tries to rise above his poor economic condition. He cherishes a desire to become a farmer like others and cultivate his own land. He knows that in caste-society the untouchables are not allowed to possess a land of their own even then he makes an attempt, at least thrice before his landlord to give him useless piece of land on rent but everytime he is rejected. Accidentally, he has found a pair of bullocks which had been lost in a forest. He rears them in the hope that one day he would use them in ploughing his own land but he is bitterly disappointed. The landlord is not entirely inclement in this matter but his old mother who has got dominant hands in the affairs of the family tells him that such thing is not traditional and an untouchable should not muster courage to make such a demand. If he does so, he is surely an arrogant person because an untouchable who has been living in such a destitute and landless condition should not aspire to become a farmer. The traditional society which is full of landlords is tyrannical and inhuman. Its prosperous people suffer from a sense of false superiority and cannot tolerate any change. The sparks of revolution are found in the hearts of Bakha and Choma but their voices of protest are suppressed.

Choma is left heartbroken at the behaviour of his landlord. He further thinks of acquiring government land but he fears that he may lose his wages from Sankappayya, the landlord who may not like his attempt to grow anything of his own. He is surrounded on all sides in such a society and his chances to come out of it are almost nothing. He becomes sad and dejected at heart but he cannot forgo his desire to become self-dependent. His beating of drum sometimes becomes reckless and loud and it is symbolic of the agony and also the fury of his heart. In a state of despair and anger he almost breaks the front legs of his oxen so that others may not use them if he is deprived of such an opportunity.

In *Untouchable* and also in *Choma's Drum* the caste-based society is the root cause of the dreadful plight of the untouchables. The members of such society are callous and cruel. They are responsible for the misery and poverty of the untouchables. Such society becomes an object of severe attack in these novels. In *Choma's Drum* it is divided into two parts, the old traditional society which follows religious and social distinction and the modern society which observes economic distinction. Exploitation of the poor and the weak like the untouchables is the main purpose of men holding superior position. The old society is represented by Sankappayya's old mother and Sankappayya himself who accepts the idea of his mother. The modern society is represented by Michael who is owner of the coffee estate. The poor labourers who are mostly untouchables work under him in the unhealthy conditions of the coffee garden and are badly exploited.

Both the novelists portray "the evils of a decadent and perverted orthodoxy".[8] Anand, the supporter of the leftist peace movement seems to be more aggressive in his *Untouchable*. "In writing of the pariahs and the bottom dogs rather than of the elect and the sophisticated, he had ventured into territory that had been largely ignored till then by Indian writers."[9] Before Anand Bankims Chand's novels were romantic with their patriotic feelings. Tagore was interested in upper and middle classes and Sarat Chandra in the lower middle class. Premchand took up the problems of the Indian peasantry. Anand descended a step low in the portrait of an untouchable like Bakha and his social exploitation. In the same way Shivaram Karanth in his *Choma's Drum* deviated from the traditional ways of novel-writing and created something fresh and original. Before him in Kannada literature the novels were characterized by religious, didactic and patriotic sentiments. Shivaram started a new pattern by writing realistic novels. He took up the questions of the untouchables who were deprived of all privileges in the then society. He dived deep into contemporary social problems of the poor and the destitute. In this respect, the two writers have a like mindedness in studying the social problems of "the poorest, and lowliest and lost".[10]

Untouchable and *Choma's Drum* are both affected by the Gandhian movement for freedom. The struggle for independence was not only political but also social. Gandhi had started a fight against several social evils and the evils of untouchablity was the main target of attack. It had divided Indian society and made it weak and vulnerable. The Indian novelists of 1920s and 1930s realized that their novels could also play a vital role in this matter. Anand had gone to Gandhi Ashram and had shown his novel to the Mahatma. On his suggestions he made several modifications. Shivaram Karanth also was motivated by the political and social questions of the day and took up contemporary problems to study the relationship of man and his surroundings. In this way both the writers were able to mobilize the feelings of the underprivileged classes which were economically depressed and politically subjugated. The result was the birth of a socially purposeful literature.

Poverty of Choma breeds poverty. His five-rupee debt has risen to twenty in five years. Choma is forced to send out two of his sons for earning daily wages and thus becoming able to pay off the increasing debt. This is the beginning of the tragic break-up and scatter of the family. His younger son Guruva is converted into Christianity in order to get rid of poverty and marries a Christian girl. The eldest son Chaniya is affected by fever at the work in the unhealthy condition of the coffee garden and dies soon. Choma's daughter Belli goes to work as a labourer for returning the debts and becomes a victim of sexual exploitation like Sohini in Anand's *Untouchable*. Michael and Marvel are the two rascals responsible for this sexual act. All these things shatter Choma's faith in society and the people. For him life appears to be a curse and a meaningless thing.

Choma is further shocked to learn that the people around the pond refuse to save his youngest son Nila from being drowned. It happens simply because he is an untouchable: "Choma realized fully that the life of an untouchable is like a running sore."[11] Choma takes away the body of his dead son and he buries it unseen by anyone. He broods over the event "Instead of being an untouchable, if he had belonged to any other caste his Nila would have been saved".[12] He said, "the caste of the untouchables is an unwanted caste even to God. Why does God bring men like him into this life? And why does he torment them?"[13] Choma becomes the symbol of suppression and servility. In the end, he is seen beating the drum violently and mercilessly as never before and dies. His death is symbolic of the agony of his heart. His mad drum beating which is his inner cry is not a failure. It is the sowing of the seed of revolution whose effect shall be seen in the coming generation. Choma's drum is the drum of Shiva which is symbol of destruction and symbol of a new creation. The novel raises its voice of protest in a silent manner and refers to a change in such society in near future.

Mulk Raj Anand also in his essay "The Source of Protest in my Novels" expresses hope for a better future for these suffering people. He writes, "I have tried to look at the realities of life, hoping that each day might be a new day of happiness with a new sun, a new moon, with new people, who may inherit the good thoughts of the past, but may look to the future. This may have meant wandering through the labyrinths, but one can recognize one's own face and the faces of others not by grovelling before fixed images but by living experience of men and women through a religion based on tenderness."[14]

NOTES

1. K.R. Srinivasa Iyengar, *Indian Writing in English*, New Delhi: Sterling Publishers Pvt. Ltd., 1984, p. 335.
2. Mulk Raj Anand, *Untouchable*, (India) New Delhi: Arnold Publishers, 1970, p. 89.
3. *Untouchable*, p. 11.
4. *Ibid.*, p. 70.

5. *Ibid.*
6. *Ibid.*, p. 71.
7. *Ibid.*
8. K.R. Srinivasa Iyengar, *Indian Writing in English*, New Delhi: Sterling Publishers, 1984, p. 339.
9. *Ibid.*, p. 333.
10. Rabindra Nath Tagore, *Gitanzali*, New Delhi: MacMillan India Limited, Song No. 10.
11. Shivaram Karanth, *Choma's Drum*, Kannada Edition, Bangalore: S.B.S. Publication, Reprint, 1992, Ch. XVII, p. 79.
12. *Ibid.*, p. 78.
13. *Ibid.*, p. 79.
14. K. Venkata Reddy and P. Bayapa Reddy, *The Indian Novel with a Social Purpose*, New Delhi: Atlantic Publishers and Distributors, 1999, p. 26.

9

The Child in Modern Indian Fiction: A Comparative Study of Two Indian Novels

Gourhari Behera and *Sunita Murmu*

> [Children] are those vessels for the visionary optimism of the adult world who are felt to carry the promise of a better tomorrow.
>
> Adrian Roscoe

The representation of the child in the cultural texts of India is as old as the culture itself. Enormous importance is accorded to the child, specially the male child, in the indigenous literary traditions of India. The exploits of Krishna, the 'bal gopal' are recorded with minutest detail in the *Bhagavata Purana* and the *Mahabharata.* Similarly the *Ramayana* also provides interesting insights into the life and adventures of the child Rama. Other child figures like Prahalada and Dhruva too figure prominently in the cultural imagination of India. Even texts like Manu's *Dharmasastra* are replete with the representation of childhood where Manu accords the child a central position in the Hindu social structure. For writers who have inherited such a literary and cultural tradition "the choice of the child as the central consciousness is understandable" (Bharat, 2003, 117). A host of writers in both English and regional languages have made the child central to their novels. Bibhutibhusan Bandopadhyaya's *Pather Panchali,* Krishna Baldev Vaid's *Uska Bachpan,* Manu Bhandari's *Aap Ka Bunty,* Ganeswar Mishra's *Face of the Morning,* R.K. Narayan's

Swami and Friends, Salman Rushdie's *Midnight's Children,* Amitav Ghosh's *The Shadow Lines* and Amit Chaudhuri's *A Strange and Sublime Address* are some of the major novels where the child's perception of reality is accorded prime importance. The present paper attempts to make a comparative study of the representation of the child as an artist in a couple of modern Indian novels written in two different languages and separated by almost thirty years.

While Bibhutibhusan Bandopadhyaya's *Pather Panchali* (1929) explores the child's growth from a pre-linguistic phase to a creative phase through various psychosocial stages, Krishna Baldev Vaid's *Uska Bachpan* (1958) translated into English as *Steps in Darkness,* charts a reverse trajectory—from the linguistic creative phase to the order of silence. The use of generic categories like 'bildungsroman' and 'kunstleroman' are intentionally avoided in this paper because they are based on an altogether different conception of time and reality that these two novels do not exhibit.

Bandopadhyaya's novel, originally written in Bangla, records the birth, growth and education of its artist-protagonist Opu. The novel describes meticulously each and every stage of Opu's growth and the narrative pattern of the novel faithfully reflects the theme. Meenakshi Mukherjee points out that "the pattern of the narrative can be seen as a series of concentric circles each expanding into the next larger..." (Mukherjee, 1985, 128-29). The novel records Opu's life right from the moment when he begins comprehending the world in terms of visual, aural and sensory details. This marks the beginning of what modern psychoanalysts call the 'Imaginary Order' where the INFANT (from Latin, *infans* meaning 'non-speaker') is in an amorphous state with no boundaries to its experience of sense of need and exists as a jumble. Jacques Lacan punningly calls this state *'l'hommlette'* or 'little man' or omellete, 'a shapeless mass of egg'. This pre-linguistic state is characterized by the infant's desire to model itself upon the mother, since she is the first being with whom the infant interacts. The 'Desire of the Mother', a very significant feature of this stage, is characterized by the child's imagining himself to be the desire of the mother and also his own desire for the mother. Consequently he is drawn into the 'falsity of completion'. Both these aspects keep the child's ego-concept in a profoundly illusory state resulting in what is termed 'meconnaisance' or 'misrecognition' as opposed to 'connaisance' or 'knowledge'. This misrecognition, according to Lacan, is the foundation of subjectivity. Lacan's concept of misrecognition roughly corresponds to Piaget's idea that in a child there is no gap between the 'self' and the 'world'. The gap begins to appear with the child's initiation into the order of language or the 'symbolic order'. Once the child is situated in this symbolic order the 'Desire-of-the-mother' is replaced by the 'Name-of-the-Father'. Between these two stages minor stages like the Oedipal stage (Freud) and the 'potential space' stage (Winnicot) or the 'field of illusion' stage (Kristeva) comes into being. The later phase, i.e. the 'potential space' sows the seed of creative impulse in the child.

In *Pather Panchali,* Opu's life trajectory can be read as his journey from the 'imaginary order' to the 'symbolic' or 'semiotic order' through 'Oedipus complex' and 'potential space' stages. We enter Opu's world almost at the beginning, of the novel when we see him attempting to master language. But this language is shapeless and incomprehensible:

> Sometimes he laughed to himself. Sometimes he chattered away in a language no one could understand. (Bandopadhyaya, 1999, 40)

The novel constantly refers to Opu's physical attachment to his mother, Shorbojaya. His recurring attempts at clinging on to her sari so that she does not go away from him are powerfully portrayed in the novel:

> Opu twisted her sari round in his hand and held it even more tightly than before. 'I am not going to let go' he said defiantly. (42)

It is significant that Opu's father, Horihor, is absent during this period and the entire episode has Freudian resonance.

The events in Opu's life in the village contribute towards his journey to the 'semiotic order'. The 'imaginary order', as already been pointed out, is characterized by 'misrecognition' wherein the child is not able to distinguish between reality and its representation. Opu's wonder at discovering the 'reality' of the hare is an interesting example,

> Opu had seen a picture of a hare under the letter H in the spelling reader, but had not recognized till now that a hare was a living thing that could jump and run away, and that you could see it with your eyes... A hare! A real live hare that actually jumps up before your very eyes and then runs away! It was not a picture, or even a glass doll, but a real live hare with its ears standing up.... (54)

The above passage clearly points out Opu's gradual moving away from the misrecognition syndrome. Not only Opu, but Durga, his elder sister, too has a similar experience when she looks inside the large tin box containing various kinds of coloured glass:

> What she saw she could never describe or understand. How did the real men get inside the box! (272)

This misrecognition is instrumental in the construction of the subjective self in the child in his passage to the 'semiotic order'.

Opu's growing attachment with his mother and Durga (who acts as a surrogate mother) also coincides with imagining his father as the antagonist 'other'. The more intense this image becomes, the more anxious he feels about the danger of being separated from his mother. Gradually the image of the antagonist becomes more and more vicious. He imagines his father being overpowered by an 'exultant demon':

> He felt as if some power from outside had come between him and his father. He looked at the house. It was empty, dark and hemmed in by bamboos. And then he looked at his father...the exultant demon horde had overpowered his father, and left him ineffectual and very lonely.... (253)

Opu's attempt at flying comes at a crucial point in the novel. This attempt can be read as the metaphoric flight usually associated with the artistic process. Opu's fancy for the vast unknown realm is repeatedly emphasized throughout the novel. His vision is perpetually directed outwards and his attempt to fly with the help of the vultures' eggs marks a distinct phase that can be termed, in D.W. Winnicot's phrase, the 'potential space', the source of all creativity. This stage is the result of the child's separation from the mother's body as the child enters the social world. The child here tries to replace the mother's real body with that of an alternative 'favoured object' and in Opu's case the vultures' eggs plays this crucial role. His failure to fly should not be taken as the complete failure of the artist but as a stepping-stone for his artistic growth. This particular event comes at a crucial point in the novel because it is only after this that Opu attempts at writing his own compositions.

Opu's friendship with other children of the village—Patu, Omola, Bishu, Ranu—serves as 'symbolist interaction' for him that helps him in the evolution of his creative self. The final, break from the 'Imaginary Order' is symbolically presented by the help of the storm in which Opu is caught while boating with one of his friends. Immediately after this, Opu undertakes a journey to his aunt's village. This particular journey is significant because compared to his previous journeys here he goes all by himself without his father. Whereas previous journeys had provided Opu with rich novel experiences, the latter journey is that of a mature self-dependent child. It is no mere coincidence that Shorbojaya, Opu's mother, hints at his sacred thread ceremony, the symbol of the child's initiation into the social matrix, at this point.

The last six chapters are packed with allusions to Opu's creative pursuits. He goes to the extent of stealing 'khoyar' (a dark brown powder used while eating beetel leaves) from his mother to use it as ink for writing his story. He also begins writing a play. He develops a passionate interest in maps and wants to become a scholar. Opu's interest exhibits a pattern of quest at this stage. He gets fascinated with stories of Columbus and Sidney. It slowly becomes clear that Opu's vision is always outward, gradually marching towards the realm of the unknown. Also there is a marked change in his vocabulary about himself in the final chapters. He begins considering himself a grown-up and does not relish the idea of being called a child anymore: 'I'm not a baby.... I am a grown-up now' (284).

Opu finally leaves his village. But he carries his experiences to the outside world. The 'Imaginary Order' is not completely abandoned but with Opu's entering the 'semiotic' order, the former is encroached upon by the latter. As Lacan aptly says, "although the Imaginary and the Symbolic (Semiotic) are distinct and opposed, the Symbolic (semiotic) encroaches upon the Imaginary, organizes it and gives it direction" (Lacan, quoted by Sarup 1991: 105). 'Opu', the novel says, "saw it with new eyes" (Bandopadhyaya 1999: 354).

Krishna Baldev Vaid's *Uska Bachpan* (1958), translated into English as *Steps in Darkness* (1960), is a direct antithesis of Bandopadhyaya's novel. It presents the life of Beero, a child brought up in the urban slums. The novel is a sensitive portrayal of the artist as a young impressionable boy. Beero is lonely, bewildered and in desperate need of sympathy and love. Meenakshi Mukherjee points out the difference between Beero's world and that of Opu's, "while Opu's world constantly opens out, Beero's closes in" (Mukherjee 1985: 142). One of the possible reasons that can be assigned to this difference is that whereas Opu's life blooms out in a village where he is in constant touch with the lush-green Nature, Beero grows up in an urban slum bereft of the benevolent canopy of Nature.

Our first encounter with Beero takes place when he has already lost his Imaginary Order and has not yet completely entered the 'Semiotic Order'. Throughout the novel there is an implicit suggestion that Beero wishes to regain his 'Imaginary Order', finally dissolving himself into the prenatal existence. What strikes us about Beero is his ambivalent attitude towards his mother. He does not completely hate his mother, but compared to Opu, his attachment with his mother is hardly discernable. Beero, of course, does exhibit the Lacanian 'Desire-of-the-Mother'. He contemplates:

> It must be mother...what is she looking for? He curls himself like a hedgehog. May be she is looking for him. (Vaid, 1960, 32)

At the same time he hates his mother too.

> he feels like kicking her from behind so that her head is buried in the oven and she conies to her senses. (8)

Like Opu, Beero too attempts at finding a surrogate mother, in order to cope with the shock of his separation from his mother. This he finds in Devi, his elder sister, in whom he finds the warmth of maternal love and tries to establish a physical bond with her:

> A hand gropes about for him and he almost melts into Devi's arms. His boot is soon warmed into drowsiness by the soft touch of Devi's body. He tries to roll himself up into a sort of ball to adjust himself to her lap.... Devi kisses him on the eyes and he feels he can't keep them open anymore. (32)

Beero, in Freudian terminology, has a 'Desire of the womb'. This regression results in what Karen Horney calls 'basic anxiety' (Horney, 1965, 211). Horney feels that when a child does not get love and affection he develops "a feeling of being isolated and helpless in a world conceived as potentially hostile" (211). A child, in these conditions, fails to relate himself to others and develops strategies to cope with the environment and unconsciously diverts his energies towards alleviating his basic anxiety. Moreover, psychological survival, one of human beings' basic needs, includes need for safety, love, belonging, self-esteem and self-actualization. These needs, when frustrated, produce neurotic conditions. The child's growth is arrested and he is alienated from his real self. Thus, in Vaid's novel, Beero's growth is arrested and he develops strategies to get back to the 'Imaginary Order' leading to regression. Yet Beero is an artist. He often soars high into the realm of imagination. His passion for kites soaring high on the sky "till it is almost like a star" (Vaid, 1960, 59) and his attempt at composing stories about Phoolrani and the king are instances that highlight his creative urge. But all his creative endeavours fail because he lacks the capacity to 'belong'. Also, unlike that of Opu, there is an absence of the 'symbolic interaction' in Beero's case. We see, moreover, that while Opu loves playing with his friends Beero shows no such interests. He prefers solitude. Eric Erickson, while commenting on the importance of 'play' in children says:

> The child's play is the infantile form of the human ability to deal with experience by creating model situations and to master reality by experience and planning. (Erickson, 1965, 183-84)

Erickson goes on to say that a child made insecure by a secret hate or fear against the natural protectors is able to use the protective sanction of an understanding adult to regain his strength. In Beero's case, he is even deprived of a protective and understanding adult. Moreover Beero is even deprived of the 'potential space' or the 'field of illusion' that we had seen in Opu's case because of the hostile surroundings. This automatically results in his failure to take any consistent imaginative flights.

Beero, compared to Opu, takes a reverse trajectory—from the order of language and creativity to the pre-linguistic order. Right in the beginning Vaid gives us the impression that Beero was already in the order of language: "Beero is familiar with all, these words..." (Vaid, 1960, 10). Beero's only comfort, Devi, too moves away from him with Naresh. The only avenue left for him to enter the 'prelinguistic' Imaginary Order is through death. At the end of the novel Beero tries strangulating himself, but survives and thus his quest remains unsuccessful. His attempt at regaining the 'prelinguistic' order, compared to Opu's passage to the semiotic order, is a failure. Vaid's novel, thus, is a powerful portrayal of the child protagonist whose artistic urge fails because of adverse circumstances into which he is born. Beero's tragedy helps the reader to locate the seed of artistic failure in a child. The theme of lost childhood, one of Vaid's favourite concerns, is effectively presented in the novel. *Steps in Darkness,* in fact, is a path-breaking novel because "the Vaid hero makes his first appearance in this novel" (Jaidev quoted in Paranjape, 1997, 223). Beero again appears in *Gujra Hua Jamana* (1981) where he is no more a child but an adolescent trying to cope with violence, both internal and external.

Although a comparative study of both the child characters, Opu and Beero, has shown opposite trajectories of development, their creators still resort to the stereotypical portrayal of the child—the child as the innocent creature whose development into an adult, either good or corrupt, depends on the external surroundings. Thus both the novels presume a romantic notion of childhood. Opu grows into a mature creative child because of various positive psycho-social factors, but Beero turns out to be a 'problem child' exhibiting regression due to a hostile and non-conducive psycho-social ambiance.

A comparative study of both the novels showed how both the authors, by making children their protagonists, have thrown immense light on how children perceive reality and what factors lead them towards maturity. It has been shown that children grow up into 'integrated selves' when circumstances are conducive but fail to do so when conditions are adverse. Many interesting ideas can emerge in the discussion regarding the representation of the child in fiction. Why, for instance, does an adult author choose to make his protagonist a child? Is it pure nostalgia? Or is the author trying to make the readers perceive the world through the child's eyes because in the child's mind all things happen in a timeless continuum of nearly pure significance? Is it that the reader seeks nothing so much as the reintegration of the honesty and selfless immediacy of the child? These questions, though difficult to answer, do stir our intellect. None-the-less the entire issue of the representation of the child in Indian fiction, especially in the postcolonial context, deserve critical attention considering the fact that the child figures prominently in some of the major literary works of our times and the importance that is paid to the child in the cultural matrix of India.

REFERENCES

Bandopadhyaya, Bibhutibhusan. (1999) *Pather Panchali,* (tr. T.W. Clark and Tarapada Mukherjee). New Delhi: Harper Collins.

Bharat, Meenakshi. (2003) *The Ultimate Colony: The Child in Postcolonial Fiction.* New Delhi: Allied Publishers.

Erickson, Eric. (1965) *Childhood and Society.* Victoria: Jossey-Bass Publishers.

Horney, Karen. (1965) *Neurosis and Human Growth.* London: Routledge.

Kristeva, Julia. (1980) *Desire in Language.* New York: Columbia University Press.

Mukherjee, Meenakshi. (1985) *Realism and Reality: The Novel and Society in India.* Delhi: OUP.

Paranjape, Makarand. (1997) *Nativism: Essays in Criticism.* New Delhi: Sahitya Akademi.

Piaget, Jean. (1967) *The Child's Conception of the World.* London: Trubner & Co. Ltd.

Sarup, Madan. (1991) *Jacques Lacan.* Toronto: University of Toronto Press.

Vaid, Krishna Baldev. (1962) *Steps in Darkness.* New York: Orion Press.

10

Ontology of Language: Rabindra Nath Tagore's *Gitanjali* and Paul de Man's Theory of Rhetorical Reading

Rajesh Babu Sharma

Paul de Man was the most rigorous practitioner of deconstructive readings. Though Jacques Derrida is generally considered to be the originator of Deconstruction, yet this is only partly true. Unaware of what Derrida was doing in philosophy, Paul de Man was practicing deconstructive readings of all kinds of texts, including that of literary text. What Derrida was doing at the level of theory, de Man was doing at level of practice. In the field of literary studies, there is no parallel to Paul de Man as far as deconstructive readings of literary texts go. Through his rhetorical readings de Man exposed the hollow nature of linguistic meaning. De Man considered that Language deceives one and all, it deceives writer, the reader, and its claim to preferentiality is equally illusionary. In his celebrated article "The Epistemology of Metaphor" (1978), de Man claimed that all the essence and value of abstract ideas or of material things or of human beings is only in language, in words. Language in its very nature is metaphorical, and metaphor (language) is the basis of all essence and truth value. These so-called radical claims of deconstruction do disturb the logocentric nature of western metaphysics. But in the eastern philosophy the void, the vacuity of language was experienced long back, since the times of creation of the *Vedas*. The human being is located in and yet beyond the language. Language is constructive and deconstructive as the metaphor is creative and yet the illusion of creativity. The empirical nature of Western knowledge systems always had problems in comprehending the Eastern view of language which was always more inclusive. And that is why one should not be surprised when de Man says, "Of Eastern philosophies no more is known than what Holderlin said in the mysterious poem *Der Ister*" (de Man 1983, 253). In this paper I attempt to compare the ontology of language in Paul de Man's literary theory and Rabindra Nath Tagore's great literary creation—*The Gitanjali.*

In his readings of literature, de Man has concentrated on the language, on the medium of literature, because it is language that is in ontological relation with literature. While discussing the form, de Man has not discussed the literary form in the usual sense of the term. The literary form in a very general sense includes lexis, syntax, phonology, meter, music, etc. But these all originate from a common entity called language. Language includes all of these, and all of these constitute language. While discussing language, most of the de Manian theory is concerned with the nature of language, especially its rhetorical and tropological nature.

To some extent, the nature of everyday language and of literary language is the same, in the sense that both share the non-referential nature of language. The referentiality of language is not inherently present in the language, it is generated by the temporality and the consciousness, and the consciousness too is temporal. We can never be certain about the meaning either in the everyday language or in the literary language. The discrepancy exists in the everyday language "...in the impossibility of making the actual expression coincide with what has to be expressed, of making the actual sign coincide with what it signifies. It is the distinctive privilege of language to be able to hide meaning behind a misleading sign, as we hide rage or hatred behind a simile" (de Man 1983, 11).

This may suggest that the speaker is consciously involved in the act of hiding meaning, that the speaker is the co-accused alongwith the language in misleading the reader. The above statement is made by de Man in the context of structuralist conception of language and the subject. For de Man idea of language in structuralism is different from the earlier concepts of language. The non-referentiality of the linguistic medium is inherent in the language.

> It is the distinctive curse of all language, as soon as any kind of interpretational relation is involved, that it is forced to act this way. The simplest of wishes cannot express itself without hiding behind a screen of language that constitutes a world of intricate inter subjective relationships, all of them potentially inauthentic. (de Man 1983, 11)

The contingent nature of language becomes so heavy upon the communicative competence of the subject involved in communication that it becomes almost difficult to say anything with certainty about the meaning making capability of linguistic communication.

> In the everyday language of communication, there is no *a priori* privileged position of sign over meaning or of meaning over sign; the act of interpretation will always again have to establish this relation for the particular case at hand. The interpretation of everyday language is a Sisyphean task, a task without end and without progress, for the other is always free to make what he wants differ from what he says he wants. (de Man 1983, 11)

Why language is incapable of any origination? This question needs to be answered to understand the ontological basis of literary works. In an article "The Intentional Structure of Image", first published in 1960, translated and reprinted in *The Rhetoric of Romanticism* (1984), de Man asserts that language in general and poetic language in particular is unlike the other natural entities, which have their own independent existence. As against the natural objects, the idea and the medium through which the idea is expressed do not have their own existence; their existence is dependent on the natural objects. Thus both are unreal, existing only through the unreliable, and inauthentic consciousness, which in mutually destructive relationship depends for its existence on language. The difference between the natural objects and the language should make the critics and interpreters aware of the mistake of analogical identity.

> How do flowers originate? They rise out of the earth without the assistance of imitation or analogy. They do not follow a model other then themselves which they copy or from which they derive the pattern of their growth. By calling them *natural* objects, we mean that their origin is determined by nothing but their own being. Their becoming coincides at all times with the mode of their origination: it is as flowers that their history is what it is, totally defined by their identity. There is no wavering in their existence: existence and essence coincide in them at all times. (de Man 1984, 4)

The essence of the natural objects is different from the essence of the language. The essence of language is that it does not have any essence, it is only by its existence in temporality that its essence is knowable. The authenticity of the poetic language is that it is inauthentic from the beginning. It is capable of origination, but the origination is in the space between the sign and signification.

> ...it is in the essence of language to be capable of origination, but of never achieving the absolute identity with itself that exists in the natural object. Poetic language can do nothing but originate anew over and over again; it is always constitutive, able to posit regardless of presence but, by the same token, unable to give a foundation to what it posits except as an intent of consciousness. (de Man 1984, 6)

Thus, the language, which is perceived to be the depository of essence, turns out to be only tropological and figural. And those figures which are generally considered to be effective in communicating the essence are in fact illusionary and those which are considered to be prosaic are closer to the illusionary nature of the essence. The illusionary nature of essence is closely linked with the very nature of language, that is the tropological nature of language. In one of his seminal articles "The Epistemology of Metaphor" first published in *Critical Enquiry* (13-30) in 1978, de Man reinterprets the three philosophers Locke, Condillac, and Immanuel Kant, to bring out the tropological nature of the essence, the idea, and the substance.

Locke's *Essay Concerning Human Understanding* can be taken up first. Locke is generally bracketed with empirical philosophical traditions but that is too naive approach to Locke's ideas. De Man reads Locke's *Essay* and finds that Locke was always aware of the power of the tropological language in the sense that tropes can delude us to any extent with regard to their referentiality.

De Man first discusses simple ideas in Locke's theory of ideas. But Locke himself says that simple ideas are undefinable. "The names of simple ideas are not capable of any definitions" (Locke bk 3, 26, qtd. in 17). Taking up the first example of "motion" which is defined as "passage", but "passage" is not a definition but translation. And even the word "translation" in German *Ubersetzen* comes from Greek translation *metaphorein.* So translation is metaphor. Second example of 'light' too plays truant when we search for meaning and definition. Locke "takes pains to explain that the word 'light' does not refer to the perception of light and that to understand the causal process by which light is produced is not at all the same as to understand light" (de Man 1978, 17).

Even the value of substance is figural and not actually composed of the so-called inherent value. De Man takes the example of "gold", and says, "Gold not only has a color and a texture, but it is also soluble" (19). The whole issue is not of constitutive properties in substances or by extension in literature, the issue is of attaching value.

> Properties it seems do not properly totalize, or rather they totalize in a haphazard and unreliable way. It is indeed not a question of ontology, of things as they are, but of authority, of things as they decreed to be. And this authority cannot be vested in any authoritative body, for the free usage of ordinary language is carried,

> like the child, by wild figuration which will make mockery of the authoritarian academy. (de Man 1978, 19)

The issue of inherent and superficially added properties becomes more intense and grave when de Man discusses the example of "Man". What is the essence of man? Is it the outward appearance or the inward soul or being? If it is only outward then we are not different from other creatures. But if the humans are defined by the inward soul, then the issue of killing of a monstrous child is also to be investigated. We define the monstrous births only because they are not shaped the way we perceive the humans, even though they may have the perfect human soul—they become monsters and are killed for being outwardly "defective". Thus humans are not humans whether we take them from outside or inside.

What de Man stresses is that all subjectivity, all consciousness, all knowledge can originate only in language. Hence, the ontology of language defines the ontology of every phenomenon that consciousness constructs through language. And as language is an inauthentic medium to know the authenticity of human existence, the authentic knowledge of any thing always deludes us.

> The ironic language splits the subject into an empirical self that exists in a state of inauthenticity and a self that exists only in the form of a language that asserts the knowledge of this inauthenticity. This does not, however, make it into an authentic language, for *to know inauthenticity is not the same as to be authentic.* (de Man 1983, 214, italics mine)

Now I take a celebrated text of an author who is deeply immersed in Eastern philosophy to make sense of the ontology of language. Rabindra Nath Tagore's *Gitanjali* is a collection of song offerings numbering about one hundred three poems. These were originally published in Bengali, later these were collected in a single volume called *Gitanjali.*

> This is the underlying idea in *Gitanjali.* The life-affirming love of God for all men, the sensual love between man and woman, the love of a mother for her

> child, the discovery of nature as a gift of God—these facets of the basic idea are inter woven throughout the book, which was composed primarily in praise of God... *Tagore offers in these poems his concept of the ideal human being—a creative, artistic, and socially active being.* ("Germany's Reaction to *Gitanjali*" in Tagore 289)

The celebrated theme of the collection thus is love of human beings to God and vice-versa, prayers to be in the presence of God and for His blessings. It is claimed that it is a collection of songs which are original and give a message of universal love towards God, human beings and Nature. It is a collection of "profoundly sensitive, fresh, and beautiful verse" by a consummate artist who "has made his poetic thought, expressed in his own English words, a part of the literature of the West" (Nobel Prize Citation *Gitanjali* 301).

The *Gitanjali* in fact celebrates the void between the consciousness and the world around, between the word and the intent, between the human and God, between the prayer to be with Being and the reality of non-presence of any such Being. Such is the undertone of these poems that this void, this space, this gap, this disjunction between language and its referent, between the being and Being becomes the central theme of the poem. We can begin to see this when the purposiveness of the prayers to God is put in question in the poems in which the poet prays for the blessings of God, for the presence of God. In song no. 47, the poet insists that he should not be disturbed in his sleep even if God comes in his presence. This is very bewildering proposition because so far the poet has been praying the presence of God, but now he asks not to be disturbed because he is sleeping.

> If the sound of his steps does not wake me,
> do not try to rouse me, I pray.
> I wish not to be called from my sleep
> by the clamorous choir of birds,
> by the riot of wind at the festival of morning light.
> *Let me sleep undisturbed even if*
> *my lord comes of a sudden to my door.*
>
> (Poem no. 47, Tagore 103 italics mine)

There is no romantic conception of the singing birds, as is in the Romantic literature, for Tagore it is "clamorous choir of birds". The wind sound is also not musical, it is not soothing, it is "the riot of wind". The poet is perhaps aware of the clamorous sounds of this world, that is why repeatedly the silence becomes the mode of his prayer. If the being can be united with Being it is through silence, silence which is empty of all meanings and sounds, silence which cannot be interpreted by language. The poet is certain of His presence but the presence is in dream and that is the reason that he doesn't want to be disturbed from the sleep because if he comes to senses, God's presence may not be seen. He wants to meet Him "When he stands before me like a dream/emerging from darkness of sleep" (*Gitanjali* 105).

The prayer for the parousia fails because it is in words and the words cannot be relied, they always cause the disruption between the prayer and God. The poet intends to sail to infinity, to that infinite space which is eternal, which is no country and to no end. When such a journey begins the subject wants to sing melodies "free as waves", "free from all bondage of words". This is very disturbing that Tagore suspects words, the words which create his songs, his prayers to God.

> Early in the day it was whispered that
> we should sail in a boat, only thou and I,
> and never a soul in the world would know
> of this our pilgrimage to no country and to no end.
>
> In that shoreless ocean, at thy silently listening smile
> *my songs would swell in melodies, free as waves,*
> *free from all bondage of words.*
>
> (Poem no. 42, Tagore 93, italics mine)

It is not that there is more or less experience than what the language can express. It is the disjunction between language and the experience that the language cannot express. It is the linguistic nature of the experience that the experience itself becomes non-existent. The moment the phenomenality of the experience is perceived in its genesis, the experience becomes in fact linguistic. It is in this sense that the medium and the idea are similar. It is in their origin that the medium and the experience share the common property of the language, that is their figurative nature. Now if the prayers (which are considered essential) are figurative, the essence of the prayers becomes the metaphorical essence. To avoid the figurative nature of the medium, the poet intends to offer his prayers in silence, because this is the only way that he can say his prayers. But silence itself is no language in de Manian sense of the term, and the moment silence is conceived in terms of language, it too will become figurative and will meet the fate of other experiences which are essentially linguistic in nature.

The theme of silence is repetitious throughout the poems. The silence vibrates, if the silence can, throughout the longings of the poet. But the longing of the being to be one with God cannot be through the medium in which the subject has written the poetry. The poet wants to offer the whole world to God. The poet desires that his senses and mind all unite together in the prayer of God, but the possibility of any such union is doubted, and the doubt is not because of any lack of sincerity or urgency on the part of the poet. The doubt has been caused by the medium, the medium of language.

Let all my songs
gather together their diverse strains
into a single current and flow to a sea of silence
in one salutation to thee.

(Poem no. 103, Tagore 257, italics mine)

From the very inception, all creativity, all consciousness, is deconstructed, only the "Deity of the ruined temple" will remain and nothing else.

Many new images are built by masters
of cunning art and carried to the holy stream
of oblivion when their time is come.

Only the deity of the ruined temple remains
unworshipped in deathless neglect.

(Song no. 88, Tagore 225, italics mine)

Gitanjali is the perfect example of naming the void between the sign and meaning. The recurrent assertion of silence is in fact the clear indication what Tagore thought of or felt of linguistic medium. Tagore is fully aware of the silence of language that is why he again and again prays for silence, and not in silence. Whereas de Man was afraid to take such conception of language of religious texts, particularly that of the Bible, Tagore had no problem to assert the silence of language even in religions prayers. The concept of deconstruction has very limited and timid application in Western theory and philosophy. The eastern philosophy is deconstructive in its real sense, and the term deconstruction is an apt one for the eastern knowledge of positivity in negativity. Whereas for de Man and the other deconstructors of his class this is *avant garde* theory of knowledge, for the eastern, it is the very basis of life and creation. For us living and non-living have little difference in the deeper sense of the term. This empirical habit of a Westerner becomes the cause of timidity when the radical notion of deconstruction is applied to God and religion. De Man in an interview with Robert Moynihan sounds like an escapist when the interviewer asked if his radical deconstructive readings could be applied to the Bible. *"There are always ironic readings possible, though just what such a reading of the Bible would be. I'd prefer not to think about. Don't ask me that"* (Moynihan 142, italics mine). To another question by Moyniham, "Is your intention to take the 'divine' out of reading?" de Man very forcefully answers,

> Yes, I intend to take the divine out of reading. The experience of the divine is one that is totally conceivable, but which I don't think is compatible with reading. One of the best theoretician of irony, Friedrich Schelegel, after having said about irony some of the most astute things that anybody has ever said about it, including Kierkegaard, and, I guess, Plato to some extent, did indeed go over to a certain mode of belief and adopted a religious life. He did not after that continue as a reader. (Moynihan 143)

So, either one can be a rigorous reader or a believer in God. The two are incompatible for de Man. That is not so for Tagore. In fact, one cannot believe in God, if one believes in meaning, that is *Maya,* of language. To believe in God, one need to disbelieve in meaning. That is the kind eastern view. In the eastern system of religion, God is demystified, decanonized, and stripped of all linguistic vanities. And this is the response to the statement of de Man that I quoted in the beginning of the article, wherein de Man claims that nothing is known of the eastern philosophies.

REFERENCES

de Man, Paul. "The Epistemology of Metaphor," *Critical Inquiry* 5:1, Autumn 1978, 13-30.

———. *Blindness and Insight: Essays in the Rhetoric of Contemporary Criticism.* 2nd ed. London: Methuen, 1983.

———. *The Rhetoric of Romanticism.* New York: Columbia University Press, 1984.

Tagore, Rabindra Nath. *Gitanjali.* Kolkata: UBS, 2003.

11

Whitman, Eliot, and the *Bhagavadgita*

Rajnath

A comparative study of Whitman and Eliot should be worthwhile for several reasons. Historically speaking, they are the two most important American poets with their large followings and widespread influences. Both have evinced tremendous interest in Indian thought and literature. And, in a still narrower context, both have been influenced by the *Bhagavadgita*, the epitome of Indian philosophy and religion.[1] In the present essay I am concerned to demonstrate the significance of the *Gita* in the writings of these two poets. Particularly important for my purposes are Whitman's "Song of Myself" and Eliot's *Four Quartets*, as it is in these poems that the *Gita* philosophy has been used extensively.

Attempts have been made to explicate both "Song of Myself" and the *Four Quartets* in the light of Christian mysticism.[2] Hence we shall have to decide whether it is the *Gita* philosophy or Christian mysticism that best explains the poems under consideration. And to arrive at this decision it is necessary to examine the differences, if any, between the *Gita* and the Christian mystical works. Of the latter the best-known are the works of St John of the Cross, the Spanish Christian mystic of the sixteenth century.

Even a cursory glance at the *Gita* and the works of St John of the Cross will reveal to us that the *Gita* philosophy is far more comprehensive than Christian mysticism. According to the *Gita* there are three ways of approaching God, the way of knowledge (*jnanayog*), the way of devotion and love (*bhaktiyog*), and the way of action (*karmayog*). The first places emphasis on contemplation, the second on faith, and the third on action. In point of fact, the *Gita* philosophy reminds one of the Platonic philosophy with its emphasis on natural aptitude. Owing to the differences in parentage and ambience, different people in the world develop different personalities. The three different ways of establishing communion with God suit different people, and a person can choose the way that suits him best. Whatever way he chooses, he arrives at the same destination.

If there is one thing that stands out in the *Gita,* it is desirelessness that cuts across all the three approaches. Thus the way of contemplation requires renunciation of worldly objects, but if a person has only outwardly renounced them and craves for them in his heart of hearts, his contemplation is incomplete (III, 6)[3] and hence not conducive to the union with God. Similarly one's devotion to a personal god may stem from one's desire for certain worldly objects; if so, one's devotion is incomplete. And, of course, a person following the path of action will have to act without any desire for the fruit of action (II, 47).

Krishna says unequivocally that complete negation of action is impossible (III, 5), because even for bodily existence one will have to indulge in action (III, 8). So true renunciation is not the renunciation of action but of the fruits of action, and a true sanyasin is one who performs his duties without any personal attachment. Though there are three ways to God, there is little doubt that it is the way of action that has been idealized by Krishna. "The renunciation of works" says Krishna "and their unselfish performance both lead to the soul's salvation. But of the two, the unselfish performance is better than renunciation" (V, 2). Hence Radhakrishnan is right when he says that the *Gita* is "a mandate for action" and that "the *Gita* asks us to live in the world and save it".[4] In the *Gita* there is no dichotomy between the Divine world and the physical world, as the latter is only a manifestation of the former.

When we come to Christian mystics, particularly St John of the Cross, we find that their emphasis falls upon contemplation, not action, and that worldly objects are reckoned by them only a hindrance. Unlike the *Gita* philosophy, Christian mysticism does not recognize the existence of God in worldly phenomena. Hence St John's belief that the soul "has gradually to deprive itself of desire for all the worldly things which it possessed, by denying them to itself."[5] According to the *Gita* it is possible for the human soul to transcend the desire for worldly objects without denying them to itself, nay while remaining closely associated with them. But for St John, "the soul cannot be possessed of the divine union, until it has divested itself of the love of created beings."[6] There is in Christian mysticism a dichotomy of body and soul, as God is imagined only as transcendent, not both transcendent and immanent as in the *Gita.*

When we examine "Song of Myself" and the *Four Quartets* with the differences between the *Gita* philosophy and Christian mysticism in mind, we find that it is the *Gita* philosophy that best explains Whitman's poem, while Eliot's poem is best explained in the light of Christian mysticism. Christian mysticism can be compared to the way of knowledge (*jnanayog*) as set forth in the *Gita,* but firstly the main drift of the *Gita* is action, not knowledge or contemplation, and secondly, though Christian mysticism is subsumed in the *Gita* philosophy, the *Gita* philosophy with its emphasis on action cannot be completely absorbed in Christian mysticism.

James E. Miller has sought to explain "Song of Myself" in the light of Christian mysticism by comparing the five stages of the poet's spiritual journey to the five stages described by Christian mystics.[7] But the failure of Miller is evident from the fact that he calls Whitman's mysticism in "Song of Myself" "inverted mystical experience". Miller's main problem, which I think he fails to resolve, is that he purports to explain the poem in terms of Christian mysticism and at the same time to find explanation for the emphasis on physical reality that Whitman places. But there will be no such problem if one approaches the poem in the light of the *Gita* philosophy where

God is viewed both transcendent and immanent. This dual nature of God in the *Gita* is clear from the following quotations:

> He who knows Me, the unborn, without beginning, also the mighty lord of the worlds, he among mortals, is undeluded and freed from all sins. (X, 3)
>
> I, O Gudakesa [Arjuna], am the self-seated in the hearts of all creatures. I am the beginning, the middle, and the very end of beings. (X, 20)

God pervades all worldly phenomena, sentient and insentient. (In chapter X Krishna says that he is present in such insentient objects as the ocean and the mountain.) Hence it is not necessary for one trying to establish union with God to shun them, or withdraw from them. On the contrary, one can approach God through the physical reality. In fact, the protagonist of "Song of Myself" places considerable emphasis on human body, as in the following lines:

> I do not press my fingers across my mouth
> I keep as delicate around the bowels as around the head and heart
> Copulation is no more rank to me than death is.
> I believe in the flesh and the appetites
> Seeing, hearing, feeling are miracles, and each part and tag of me is a miracle.[8]

Seeing, hearing, feeling, and other aspects of the physical reality are miracles, because they are a means to the communion with the Divine reality.

Since Whitman accepts the immanence of God, he has a very sympathetic attitude towards the downtrodden, the vicious, the vulgar as well as towards animals and birds (12-13). God pervades the great as well as the small, the virtuous as well as the vicious. He does not consider even the tortoise "unworthy because she is not something else". When he assumes the role of Krishna in the *Gita* he enters all, foolish and wise, old and young, male and female.

> I am of old and young, of the foolish as much as the wise

Regardless of others, even regardful of others,
Maternal as well as paternal, a child as well as a man,
Stuffed with the stuff that is coarse and stuffed with the stuff
that is fine.... (pp. 37-38)

In his make-up Whitman the poet is like Krishna subsuming in himself the entire cosmos, and all the aspects of it, good and bad.

It has been said that the "I" in "Song of Myself" is Krishna.[9] But the protagonist is Krishna only metaphorically, not literally; in other words, he has only some of the characteristics of Krishna and as such cannot be completely identified with the latter. After all, he is only a creator and not the creator. And, in fact, the speaker of the poem says in so many words that he is a poet who sings of all kinds of worldly phenomena from the carpenter and the lunatic to the yankee girl and the canal boy: "Of these one and all I weave the song of myself." Both in the East and the West the poet has been compared to God.[10] I shall go a step further to say that the poet is more like Krishna than the Christian God, Krishna who is both transcendent and immanent. Like Krishna pervading the universe, the poet enters into all that he sees, but, again like Krishna, he transcends all individual phenomena. Thus the poet is present everywhere and nowhere. D.H. Lawrence fails to realize this when he remarks that the phrase "merging with everything" suggests that Whitman has no individuality.[11] Whitman not only merges with everything but also transcends it.

Like Whitman, Eliot was highly fascinated by the *Gita* and used it in his *Four Quartets,* particularly "The Dry Salvages". The central theme of the *Four Quartets* is the intersection of time and Eternity in the Incarnation of Christ. The theme is stated in the first of the quartets, "Burnt Norton" in the following words:

At the still point of the turning world. Neither flesh nor fleshless

> Neither from nor towards; at the still point, there the dance is
> But neither arrest nor movement. And do not call it fixity,
> Where past and future are gathered.[12]

At the point of the Incarnation, flux and fixity combine, and hence it is wrong to call it flux or fixity alone. God who is described by St. Augustine as "ever still standing" enters the flux of time at a particular point and thus the Incarnation is the meeting point of flux and Eternity.

The protagonist of "Song of Myself" goes out into the external world, while that of the *Four Quartets* withdraws from it into his own self. Since the God of "Song of Myself" is also immanent and as such exists in all worldly phenomena, the physical world is considered delightful, not despicable. But the God of the *Four Quartets* is viewed only as transcendent, and worldly reality only as a hindrance. Hence the emphasis in Eliot's poem on withdrawal from the world. This difference between Whitman's and Eliot's poems can be best explained in terms of the difference between the *Gita* philosophy and Christian mysticism. We have already observed that at the center of "Song of Myself" is the *Gita* philosophy. But at the center of the *Four Quartets* is Christian mysticism, particularly that of St John of the Cross.

It is hardly possible to exaggerate the influence of St John of the Cross on the *Four Quartets*. The poem is throughout charged with the vocabulary of the Spanish mystic. Terms like "Old man", "darkness", "wait", "empty" which occur frequently in the *Four Quartets* remind one at once of St John of the Cross. Eliot goes to the extent of referring in "Burnt Norton" to the mystic ladder with ten steps described in *The Dark Night of the Soul*. One can easily give numerous instances from the *Four Quartets* which have parallels in St John of the Cross. The two most striking instances are one each in "Burnt Norton" (the second passage of the first movement) and "East Coker" (the first passage of the third movement). In the former Eliot describes the Active Dark Night of the sense and spirit which is the subject of *The Ascent of Mount Carmel* and in the latter the Passive Dark Night of the soul which is dealt with in *The Dark Night of the Soul*. The "deprivation and destitution of all property" and the "desiccation of the world of sense" described in the former is the Active Dark Night of the sense and spirit, while the "darkness of God" in the latter is the Passive Dark Night.

It is evident from the foregoing discussion that the most dominant element in the *Four Quartets* is Christian mysticism with its emphasis on contemplation. Now we have to see whether the introduction into the poem of the *Gita* philosophy with its emphasis on action is justified.

The *Gita* appears significantly in the third section of "The Dry Salvages". The two main verses of the *Gita* that Eliot refers to are as under:

> To action alone has thou a right and never at all to its fruits; let not the fruits of action be thy motive; neither let there be in thee any attachment to inaction. (II, 47)
>
> Thinking of whatever state (of being) he at the end gives up his body, to that being does he attain, O Son of Kunti [Arjuna] being ever absorbed in the thought thereof. (VIII, 6)

The ideas contained in these verses have been used by Eliot in the following lines:

> At the moment which is not of action or inaction
> You can receive this: "On whatever sphere of being
> The mind of a man may be intent
> At the time of death"—that is the one action
> (And the time of death is every moment)
> Which shall fructify in the lives of others
> And do not think of the fruit of action.
> Fare forward. (p. 211)

The moment is not one of action or inaction in the physical sense, but the moment of illumination which is at the most a mental action. Incidentally, the moment is also "the moment in and out of time", the moment when the flux of time meets Eternity, the moment of the Incarnation and the moment of apprehending the Incarnation. As Eliot quotes only part of the second verse above, it does not make sense and, in fact, to anyone completely ignorant of the *Gita* the lines in quotation marks must be highly puzzling. But with the complete verse of the *Gita* before us we can easily make out what Eliot is driving at. A person goes to that state of being on which his mind is concentrated at the time of death.

The line in brackets, "And the time of death is every moment," seems to have baffled Eliot's critics, as no satisfactory explanation has yet been advanced. In a recent exegesis of the poem Derek Travers intimates that the moment of death completes the pattern of one's life and, therefore, it "cannot be considered as an isolated terminal point, but covers in a very real sense the whole course of each individual existence".[13] But the question is whether it is this that Krishna means. It seems critics have not bothered to find the explanation of the line in the *Gita*. The verse following the one from which Eliot quotes says:

> Therefore at all times remember Me and fight. When thy mind and understanding are set on Me to Me alone shalt thou come without doubt. (VIII, 7)

The ideal moment of death is when one dies with his thought anchored in Lord Krishna, and one should try to realize this ideal every moment in one's life and act; in other words, one should act with one's mind centered in God and such an action will be in the spirit of sacrifice to Him rather than for any personal gain. "At all times remember Me" in the above quotation becomes in Eliot's poem "And the time of death is every moment". But we must bear in mind that Krishna's emphasis fall upon the word "fight"; in other words, Krishna is telling Arjuna how to act, not just how to die or what to meditate on. In fact, Eliot's critics are not so much to blame as Eliot himself, who has changed the very complexion of the *Gita* by shifting the emphasis from action to contemplation. A poet who can imagine worldly actors including captains, men of letters, statesmen, and rulers going into the dark ("East Coker", III) is definitely going contrary to the spirit of the *Gita*. In "East Coker" Eliot writes: "For us, there is only the trying. The rest is not our business" (p. 203). And using Eliot's own language ("East Coker", III) one can say that for Eliot "the trying will be trying for the wrong thing". Eliot seems incapable of imagining a healthy worldly action that liberates the human soul from worldly fetters, the kind of action that has been prescribed by the *Gita.* According to Krishna, physical action can be bondage or freedom depending on the spirit in which it is undertaken, but to Eliot every physical action is bondage.

Using Arnold's words, Helen Gardner says that Eliot's early poetry deals with boredom and horror, while his later poetry deals with glory.[14] But the only glory that Eliot is capable of envisioning is the glory of God, not the glory of physical reality. Hence it is difficult to make out what Eliot means when he says: "And do not think of the fruit of action." What action does he mean? Is it mental action that leads to the union with God? If so, the fruit of action is not so much to be worried about. Krishna's injunction to Arjuna that he should not worry about the fruit of action has its true significance only in the context of physical action.

In the next passage Eliot addresses voyagers and seamen to tell them what their real destination is, and again we notice that he is changing the complexion of the *Gita.*

> O voyagers, O seamen,
> You who come to port, and you whose bodies
> Will suffer the trial and judgement of the sea
> Or whatever event, this is your real destination
> So Krishna, as when he admonished Arjuna
> On the field of battle. (p. 211)

Krishna's emphasis is on choice, while Eliot places his emphasis on predestination. As Harry Blamires has said, Eliot is using the word "destination" "in its less usual sense, the end or purpose for which a person or thing is destined".[15] The voyagers and seamen are being advised to be indifferent to the final outcome of their action, predetermined as it is. Moreover, the voyagers are the spiritual voyagers to whom life and death are the same, because there is always life after death and death after life. Water in the above passage, as in *The Waste Land,* is symbolic of spiritual regeneration. Thus the drowning in the sea and the Divine union will come to the same end. Eliot has again changed the complexion of the *Gita* by shifting the emphasis from physical action to spiritual union.

Of the two poets, Whitman and Eliot, it is Whitman who has got the spirit of the *Gita* right. Eliot emphasizes the glory of the Divine world to the exclusion of that of the physical world. In his poetry there is a clear dichotomy between the Divine and physical worlds which goes against the spirit of the *Gita*. Whitman, on the other hand, recognizes the glory of both the worlds which is in conformity with the spirit of the *Gita*.

NOTES

1. There is a great deal of controversy regarding the possibility of Whitman's familiarity with the *Gita* at the time of his writing *Leaves of Grass*. But considering that the poem reminded Emerson of the *Gita* (he described it as "a remarkable mixture of the *Bhagvat Ghita* and the *New York Herald*") there is every possibility that Whitman was familiar with it at the time he wrote the poem. For a discussion of the source and extent of Whitman's knowledge of the *Gita* see T.R. Rajasekharaiah, *The Roots of Whitman's Grass* (Rutherford: Fairleigh Dickinson University Press, 1970), pp. 105-08. That Eliot was familiar with the *Gita* before he took to the composition of the *Four Quartets* is evident from his remark in his essay on "Dante" (1929) that "the *Bhagavad-Gita* is the next greatest philosophical poem to the *The Divine Comedy* within my experience". *Selected Essays* (London: Faber and Faber, 1966), p. 258.
2. James E. Miller, *A Critical Guide to Leaves of Grass* (Chicago: The University of Chicago Press, 1957), pp. 6-35, and Rajnath, *T.S. Eliot's Theory of Poetry: A Study of the Changing Critical Ideas in the Development of His Prose and Poetry* (Atlantic Highlands, N.J.: Humanities Press, 1980), pp. 156-59.
3. *The Bhagavadgita,* translated with an Introduction by S. Radhakrishnan (New Delhi: Blackie, 1977). It is this translation that has been used throughout this essay.
4. *Ibid.*, pp. 66-67.

5. *The Complete Works of St John of the Cross,* ed. E. Allison Peers (London: Burns Oats and Washbourne, 1934), p. 19.
6. Eliot has used this as an epigraph to his "Sweeney Agonistes".
7. Miller, p. 7.
8. *Leaves of Grass,* ed. Carl Sandburgh (New York: The Modern Library, 1921), p. 45. Subsequent references are indicated in parentheses after each citation.
9. Rajasekharaiah, pp. 417-18.
10. As M.H. Abrams has pointed out, Coleridge has made a triple parallel of God, the human mind, and the poet. *The Mirror and the Lamp* (New York: W.W. Norton, 1938), p. 283. Anandavardhana, the famous Indian critic of the ninth century, states that "in the vast world of poetry the poet is like the Creator".
11. *Studies in Classic American Literature* (Harmondsworth: Penguin Books, 1971), p. 173.
12. *T.S. Eliot: Collected Poems* (London: Faber and Faber, 1974), p. 191. Subsequent references to the "Four Quartets" are indicated in parentheses after each citation.
13. *T.S. Eliot: The Longer Poems* (London: The Bodley Head, 1978), p. 173.
14. *The Art of T.S. Eliot* (London: Faber and Faber, 1968), pp. 79-80.
15. *Word Unheard: A Guide Through Eliot's Four Quartets* (London: Methuen, 1969), p. 109.

12

Life of a Tenant Farmer—Kamala Markandaya's *Nectar in a Sieve* and Premchand's *Godan*

Neeru Tandon

I

Comparative literature, popularly written as 'comp. lit.' is critical scholarship dealing with the literature of two or more different linguistic, cultural or national groups. Goethe proposed two terms in 1795 and 1826:

(a) Welt Literature (world literature)

(b) Vergluchend (comparative literature)

When we talk about English school of comparative literature, the name comes before us is Chasle Philatre. In 1848, in one of his letters to his sister, he wrote about comparative literatures. It was different from the singular literature. Touchstone theory is in fact nothing but comparative literature. The function of literature is to delineate. What National literature does is—alienate, but comparative literature de-alienates it. Hogo de Malitz said, comparative literature should operate in three directions:

(a) Re evaluation of history.

(b) Comparison between literatures of two languages. It also includes comparative translations.

(c) Acceptance of multilingualism.

In 1892 in Aukland, Posnett opened up the area of comparative literature in various ways. First, it was the tradition to take one author of one language and other author of other language. Posnett said that while most frequently practiced with works of different languages, it may also be performed on work of same language. He took H.H. Remax and S.S. Prawan's 'Comparative Literature—An Introduction', which is considered as Bible of the comparative literature. The main fact established by this, lies in the issue that writer lives in the society—apart from the literary forces he'll be influenced by other forces like economical, political, social, biological, cultural influences as well. The moment writer does this he goes out of the discipline. As we know, earlier comparative literature was limited to the literary influence or humanities, today's comparative literature exhibits the influence of New Criticism also as there the text is autonomous. So it has no relation with the author, context and other text by that author. It will be dealt in isolation.

Later on there emerged certain confusions and problems. Tradition believes in continuity, so it goes against the rules of New-Criticism. Comparative literature did not flourish much. Lane Cooper said, "Though I am here to be the head of comparative literature, but I'm not happy with the Norman-Clature. Rather there should be comparative study of literature".

After 1960 comparative literature gained new directions: also known as Commonwealth Literature and New Literature. But again these categories did not serve the real purpose as it includes only the literatures written in English.

In India first full fledged department of comparative literature was opened in Jadavpur. They started comparative Indian literatures. Of course India which has so many literatures in so many languages is a fit place to study comparative literature. It will create a dialogue between many languages and states. If one wants to understand Indian literature in totality, it is possible only when they stood together in comparison.

Then we come across the origin of Translation Studies. This shift is very important as we cannot be the masters of so many languages at a time: thus various literatures in translation should be available. Susan Bassnett was known for his two books, *Comparative Literature—A Critical Introduction*, 1994 (Blackwell Publications) and *Translation Studies* (Ruley in 1996). He felt and suggested strongly that comparative literature should include cultural studies as well along with translations. Amitabh Ghosh pressing upon the significance of translation in the contemporary society said, "Societies that do not translate have no future." Translation brings intellectual wealth through domestication and adaptation. Translation is called 'Parkaya Pravesh'. Soul is the same, it moves from one body of language to another. But it should be faithful to the spirit of the source text. Transliteration, Transcreation and Procreation are various terms to replace translation.

II

The famous critic Harry Levin in 1968 said, "We are wasting too much energy into discussing theory of comparative literature, rather we should use half of the energy in really comparing the literature, it would be great."

Following the said advice I have taken two major texts of the two languages: Kamala Markandaya's *Nectar in a Sieve* (English) and Munshi Premchand's *Godan* (Hindi). Both the novels deal with the rural life and the problems of tenant farmers.

According to Webster Dictionary a tenant is "a person who farms land owned by another and pays rent in cash or in a share of the crops".

In India most discussion of agriculture emphasize the tripartite division of the agricultural population into those who own the land but before 1914 did not farm it themselves; the tenant farmers, who rent the land from the owners; and the agricultural labourers, who are paid wages and lack any land other than a garden.

The life of tenant farmers is full of problems. Large families, lack of infrastructure, industrialization, lack of education, their backwardness superstition, etc. can be considered as major factors. For example, a major problem is crop loan to produce wheat; paddy etc. a farmer needs some financial assistance. Being a tenant farmer he does not have a legal right over the land, so he cannot get a loan from the bank, reason being, he is only a tenant over the land. So, he goes to a money lender who takes money at a high rate of interest and he suffers because of this.

There is a large and contentious literature on the nature and problems of peasant societies. As Oscar Wilde said, "Literature always anticipates life. It doest not copy it, but moulds it to its purpose". Over the years, literature has reflected the prevailing social issues, including farmers and labourers. This type of literature also known as 'proletarian literature' dealt with labour issues, and position and problems of people working in the farmland. Writers produced poems, songs, agitprop skits, full-length plays, sketches, short-stories and novels on subjects related to farmers and farm land in a wide variety of styles. Writers such as Ivan Vazor of Bulgaria, Garcia Torca of Spain, Louis Aragon of France, Bertolt Brecht of Germany, Nazim Hikmet of Turkey, Pablo Neruda of Cluile and Vladimir Mayakovsky and Maxim Gorky of Russia touch the life and conditions of the working class.

Father of William Shakespeare and father of John Burns (1759-96) also worked as tenant farmers. In India also, major writers have thrown light on the life of tenant farmers. *Mahesh* (1921) by Saratchandra Chatterjee is a Bengali short piece of fiction, which revolves around the life of a Muslim tenant farmer under a Hindu zamindar. In it novelist talks about the issue of Hindu-Muslim religion, but at the same time it also deals with the agrarian problems of rural India. Saratchandra's work represented rural Bengali society and he often wrote against social superstitions and oppression.

Rental Arrears (1938) (Pattabakki) written by K. Damodaran is our first play on a socio-political theme. It is the first Malayalam drama that dealt with tenant farmers and land lords who levied ruinous rents. It deals with the confrontation of tenants with the various arms of the local government in the India of 1930s.

Mulk Raj Anand in his novel *Coolie* deals with the tragic denial to a simple landless peasant of the fundamental right to happiness. Munno, had heard of how the landlord hard seized his fathers' five acres of land because the interest on the mortgage covering the unpaid rent had not been forthcoming. When the rains had been scanty and the harvest failed. In his another novel *Two Leaves and a Bud* Munno is replaced by a landless peasant Gangu who belong to a family from a Punjabi village. Gangu loses his ancestral property owing to debt and is compelled in old age to indenture (sealed agreement or contract) himself, his wife and his two children as labourers in a British owned tea-plantation in far-of Assam. Gangu presents all those baffling contrasting strains which marked the pre-independence Indian peasant character the theme of the exploitation of the peasantry by various agencies in handling adequately in his trilogy.

Sick Man (Bimar, 1941) by Sajjad Syed Zaheer is an Urdu play, which deals with the struggles of a group of Indian peasants and labourers against rent collectors in 1940.

Kalicharan Pattnayak's *Rice* (Bhate, 1944) is a play about exploitation of tenant farmers in Orissa. *So Many Hungers* (1947) by Bhabani Bhattacharya is an outstanding work on the struggle and hardships of rural Indian peasantry *Two Measures of Rice* (1948) by Takazhi Sirvasaran Pillai depicts the lives of landless labourers working in the paddy fields of northern Kerala.

There are many other novels too on such themes like *Womb of Fire* (Agnigarbha, 1978) a Bengali novel by Mahasweta Devi. This novel features the inhuman exploitation by landlords of landless labouers in tea plantations. With a focus on the Naxalbari Movements in West Bengal in the 1960's, the novel reveals the magnitude of labour exploitation and the forms of labour resistance.

Godan (1936) is a Hindi novel by Premchand. Munshi Premchand lived from 1880 to 1936 and can justly lay claim to the title of the best Hindi fiction writer ever. He was born on 31 July 1880 in a small village, Lamhi, near Varanasi. His parents named him Dhanpat Rai. He started writing at a young age. Initially, he wrote in Urdu. Later, he wrote only in Hindi. It successfully explores lives of farmers and agricultural labourers in rural Indian and pathetic story brimming with utter poverty and helplessness. This novel *Godan* deals with the dreams and ambitions of the major character Hori who is an immortal character symbolic of the peasantry of this country. Through the peasants, Premchand has portrayed the pathetic life of the rural arena. Hori is an embodiment of peasant virtue, simplicity and truth. He leads an inconsistent life with his wife Dhania and his three children. Three sons had died in infancy. She felt sad that she could not provide them proper medical facility to save their lives. She herself was thirty-six years old but her grey hair and wrinkled face, swarthy complexion, dim eye-sight tell the tale of her constant penury. Her mind would often rebel against such a state of affairs. But a few scolding from her husband would jolt her back into reality. Hori said to Dhania, "Out of scores of people in the village can you name one who has not been ejected from his land or been served with attachment orders? When your neck is being trampled under the tyrant's heel, the safest course is to keep on tickling his feet" (19).

Of their six children only three had survived—one son, Gobar, who was now sixteen years old and two daughters, Sona (12 years) and Rupa (eight years). They spend a quarter of their lives in starvation and the rest-paying unwarranted loans. The money-lenders take full advantage of their poverty and therefore take unreasonable interest from them. The money-lenders also exploit the ignorance and gullibility of the peasants. Zamindars make maximum use of the tenants and extract manual labour from them. Premchand presented a word picture: "Hori fed the bullocks and prepared a chelum for himself. He was still in debt, some three hundred rupees, and the loan was gathering interest at the rate of hundred rupees each year. Five years ago he had borrowed sixty rupees from Mangru, the money lender, to buy the bullocks. He had already paid sixty rupees as interest. The loan of thirty rupees which he had taken from Pundit Data din to plant potatoes had now jumped to a hundred. There were other loans too, and a part of the revenue still unpaid" (28). Hori thinks if things went on like this he might have to auction his house and perhaps his children would become beggars. Hori's only consolation was that he was not the only miserable man, other peasants were in the same boat, and some in fact were drowning. Jewan Mehta was so poor that he had to send beggars away empty handed. Debt lay on the village like a curse. Hori, already old, and fatigued from poverty has to do strenuous work in order to earn his livelihood. The cow he eventually gets hold of is mercilessly killed by his cruel brother Heera.

The younger generation of peasants opts for city life. For them, material prospects hold more importance than simple rural pleasures and sentimental values. Gobar, Hori's rebellious son runs away from home to Lucknow and starts working there as a labourer. After a brief span of success and glitter, as the young man comes to realize the inherent character of the city, he grows into maturity.

Hori's entire life is wedded to nature. The trees bore fruits but for others, the land yields grains but to appease the other hungry mouths. But Hori does not approve of his son Gobar's idea of shifting to the city. A typical peasant, his land is everything to him. He regards the cattle also as a member of the family. He faces many problems, commonly faced by almost every tenant farmer. He had to marry off sons too. It was bad enough if a son did not marry, but for a grown-up girl to remain unmarried was sacrilege. He had no courage to face his friends and society with an unmarried girl in the house. His daughter Sona was still in her teens. She had the body of a fully grown girl and the brains of a child, as though the woman and the child in her were struggling.

Premchand wrote sincerely about social realities, particularly the realities concerning the lives of the vast peasant masses of this country. Much accolade was heaped upon him for his empathic representation for the lowest of the low so much so that his writing was considered reactionary and ahead of the times. He depicted with a deep understanding, the tragedy and pathos of their dark lives, their rare smiles and unceasing sorrow, their frustration and hopes in his short stories also. The story of Halku in *Poos Ki Raat* offers an acute insight psyche of one such farmer. Finding it difficult to stand guard to the crop on a winter night without a blanket, Halku decides to work as a labourer instead. Even a cursory glance at the plot and treatment in the novel is sufficient to convince one about Premchand's sympathy with the oppressed farmers whom he considered at the receiving end of the unjust system, for instance Hori in *Godan* possesses all the attendant virtues of a farmer with his reticence, his fatalism and hard-working nature.

Nectar in a Sieve by Kamala Purnaiya Taylor popularly known as Kamala Markandaya aims to introduce the western students to the rural life in India and the changes which took place during the time when India was under the British rule. It is a pathetic story of a large poverty stricken Hindu family of a remote rural area in southern Indian. The story of the novel moves around Rukmani, the narrator, who reveals the miseries and sufferings of her husband Nathan a tenant farmer.

Kamala Markandaya has had the experience of living and working in villages when she was involved in social work. She understood the problems of the peasant class; saw their sufferings, their resentment to industrialization and their distrust of industrial and economic changes. Charles R. Larson, a close friend of Markandaya and a noted professor of literature, American University, Washington D.C. said in this regard. I quote,

> The wanderlust must have rubbed off on the young girl, born Kamala Purnaiya, in a small town in Mysore on 23 June 1924—she had decided, to her parents' dismay, that she wanted to become a journalist. She wrote a number of articles about social changes brought about by the war and accepted a position offered by a friend to work on what she identified as a 'progressive' magazine—when the war ended, Markandaya also began what in several places she termed 'an experiment in rural living'. The experience was limited to a few months but the impact was enormous because *Nectar in*

a Sieve was largely based on her close observations of country life.[1]

Shiv K. Kumar calls *Nectar in a Sieve* the 'Magnum Opus' of the Kamala Markandaya. He said that his novel translated into 17 languages including Russian in 1958 brought her worldwide fame. One letter—written to an American scholar—included the following remark by Richard Walse who married the Nobel Laureate Pearl Buck: "we feel strongly enough this novel of peasant life in India to think it possible that it may arouse in America something of interest in the ordinary people of India that The Good Earth did for China". Many others including the promotional material for the book also talk about the comparisons between the two works. However it can't be certified, if Markandaya had ever read Pearl Buck's novel.[2]

Kamala Markandaya depicting the life of a village does not portray the life of the big landlords but she depicts the life of the landless farmers who are also the most neglected people. Rukmani has come from a family, who own the land they till. But Nathan her husband is a landless farmer. Rao observes, "In *Nectar in a Sieve* Markandaya dramatizes the tragedy of a traditional Indian village and a peasant family assaulted by industrialization. Rukmani and Nathan, the peasant couple in a south Indian village, are the victims of the two evils, zamindari system and the industrial economy."[3]

Nageshwara Rao a reputed critic, observes, "the novel deals with the peasants, their activities, problems and anxieties, hopes and expectations, and joys and sorrows. It is therefore natural to find in it an emphasis on rural ethos and rural value systems."[4]

Nathan as a typical tenant farmer is wedded to the land and he knows no other profession except that behind the plough. He expects that with a sense of favourable seasons, he will be affluent enough to buy for himself the land he tills on lease. "While there was land there was hope for Nathan" (136). He has to live on the mercy of the zamindar. He suffers under the zamindari system.

The novel opens with the description of the condition of Nathan as a landless farmer and Rukmani (or Ruku), as she is more frequently called the daughter of the farmer who owns his land. Nathan being an industrious tenant farmer leads a life of contentment in his soil and has one dream only to have the land as his own.

The living conditions of these farmers are almost primitive. Nathan's house is a small thatched hut near a paddy field in the vicinity of a couple of similar huts. He was 'poor in everything but love and care for his wife, whom he took at the age of twelve'. Together they grew and sell grains, exchanging their crop for food at the village; Rukmani also has a fruit and vegetable patch for their own consumption. They expect their sons to carry on their age-old tradition of tilling the land, living in extended family networks and maintaining Hindu values. The couple till the land, water the plants and manure the crops in a joint venture hoping for a rich harvest. As a tenant farmer Nathan has to work for long hours everyday, even then his meager income is uncertain Rukmani pathetically ponders, "To those who live by the land there must always come times of hardship...sometimes we eat and sometimes we starve" (136).

Whether it is drought or flood, Nathan is always a tragic victim of the forces of nature. If the crops are good there is a feast if not then fast. In this chain of fasting-feasting, most of the time is occupied by fasting. It is quite obvious that Indian agriculture is a gamble of the monsoons which are unpredictable. Farmer wants balanced blessings of God Indra. Kamala Markandaya writes, "the fruit of the peasant's labour goes either to the landlord or is destroyed by the ravages of nature."

Nathan has to pay revenue for the use of land to his landlord in all circumstances. As the crops fail every year Nathan is not in a position to pay the rent continuously for years, hence his landlord orders to evacuate the land. K.R. Chandrashekaran presents the outline of the novel in the article East and West in the novel of Kamala Markandaya:

> The life of toil, an uncertainty lived by the tenant farmers of India, who comprise the bulk of the

> population represented with understanding and compassion through the simple peasant, Nathan and his family. It is the lot of Nathan to till the land which belongs to another, paying exorbitant rent for it and getting hardly a square meal a day as reward even after the best harvest.[5]

This novel focuses upon hunger, poverty, beggary, lack of family planning crime, unemployment, prostitution, the zamindari system, caste and class conflict, superstition, dowry system, low status of woman, evil of the marriage system, etc. It is also concerned with the conflicts that arise due to the industrialization of an Indian village. Nathan and Rukmani represent thousands of uprooted peasants under the industrial economy. The presentation is so emphatic that the work of fiction automatically becomes the study of a rural community. It depicts the agony of transition from the traditional agrarian mode of life to the modern industrial way. The effect of industrialization on the life of a tenant farmer and his family has been depicted very beautifully and sensibly by the novelist. The tannery destroys the life of Nathan and Rukmani; it causes pollution and destroys the atmosphere of the place. The pastures are used by the industries. Therefore, Rukmani says: "they had invaded our village with chatter and din, had taken from us the maidan where our children played and had made the bazaar prices too high for us."[6]

The renowned critic K. Venkata Reddy compares tannery with "a serpent in her (Rukmani's) Garden of Eden".[7]

The establishment of the tannery proves to be fatal for tenant farmers like Nathan and Rukmani because the land is occupied by it. It purchases the land by paying high prices. It becomes the cause of tenancy in farming, rural indebtedness, untold poverty and extreme wretchedness. It also causes the decline of natural beauty. It plays havoc with village economy and uproots a tenant farmer.

The rural people are illiterate, Rukmani as an exception knows how to read and write. She understands the importance of education and teaches her children at home because she cannot afford to send them to school. Markandaya also throws light on population problem. Nathan and Rukmani have seven children, previously Nathan and Rukmani were happy and contended but later on they find it difficult to manage their family within that limited meals as the family size is big. Markandaya talks about the inner satisfaction and immense pleasure of a tenant farmer which is again embedded in the farming. Novelist has studied the psyche of the tenant farmer in depth is clear from the following brilliant passage:

> The sowing of seed disciplines the body and the sprouting of the seed uplifts the spirit, but there is nothing to equal the rich satisfaction of a gathered harvest, when the grain is set before you in shining mounds and your hands are whitened with the dust of the good rice. (104)

It is clear that the satisfaction of a landless farmer to see his 'gathered harvest' in 'shining mounds' cannot be compared with any other treasure of the world. The concept of their happiness is very simple, based on their need of food, clothing and shelter.

Land is a source of sustenance to which the peasant depends. The earth with its familiar smell and affectionate warmth revives the sagging morale of the peasant whenever Rukmani's spirits are drooping; Nathan raises them again and again by reminding her of the fertile land. He consoles Rukmani: "Such harvests as this and you shall not want for anything" (10). But the tragedy of rural life in India is that the farmers are entirely, dependent on nature with her innate circumstances and freaks of weather. When their harvest fails owing to natural calamities, the farmers face not only starvation, but also miserable poverty that forces them to sell their small possessions in order to pay rent. This is what happened to Nathan and Rukmani. Driven by the cruel fate or hostility of the landlords, the peasant family has to relinquish the land which was their only hope and which they were cultivating for decades and also to which they were deeply attached. Nathan hoped that he would own the land he tilled, but in vain. Zamindar sent Sivaji to realize the rent of the land. Which could not be paid owing to the failure of the crop. One year it rained beyond limits, and the following year there was no rain. Therefore Nathan sold the pots and pans, the food and the bullocks, even then, the money (Rs. One Hundred and Twenty Five rupees) was not even the half he had to pay. Rukmani sums up the life of a peasant, when she says:

> Hope and fear. This forces that hugged is first in one direction and then in another and which one was stronger no one could say—fear, constant companion of the peasant...fear, fear of the dark future, fear of the blackness of death. (110)

Their equation More Rice to Sell becomes No Rice to Sell and finally No Rice to Eat. And then at the fag end of his life he is cruelly dispossessed of his land. When the tannery owners pay good price, the zamindar sells all his lands and Nathan and many others like him have to go landless. He wishes to see his sons besides him to teach them the ways of the earth how to sow, to transplant, to reap, to know the wholesome from the rotten, the unwelcome reed from the paddy. Situation changes, they become landless and not Rukmani and Nathan helplessly wait for the employment of their sons at the tannery. The tenant farmer could not save one of his sons from being killed at the tannery and another dying of starvation. Their daughter Era takes to prostitution in order to survive. Once Rukmani divides rice into 24 small parts to feed the entire family for so many days. In utter helplessness these tenant farmers did what was the last option for them; that is to migrate to a city as labourers as stone breakers. Rukmani feels dejected and broken. She utters:

> This hut with all its memories was to be taken from us for it stood on land that belonged to another and the land itself by which we lived. It is cruel thing, I thought. They do not know what they do to us. (137)

The city life offers them nothing. And they try to save money so that they could go back to the village and settle down there in peace. But even this was difficult.

Finally Nathan dies of privation and disease. A man like Nathan, who throughout his life produced food for others, suffers to such a great extent that could provoke pity in any heart. Rukmani paints a very tragic picture of hunger—

> Thereafter we fed on whatever we could find; the soft ripe front of the prickly pear, a sweet potato or two, blackened and half rotten, thrown away by some prosperous hand sometimes a crab that Nathan managed to catch near the river. Early and late my sons ruined the country side, returning with a few bamboo shoots, a stick of sugarcane left in some deserted field, or a piece of coconut picked from the gutter in the town...for every edible plant or root there was a struggle a desperate competition that made enemies of friends and past an end to humanity. (87)

This word picture is immaculately frank and ruthlessly realistic without any shallow idealization. Rukmani's words reflect the injured feelings and helplessness of thousands of Indian poor peasants who are confronted with the new encompassing industrial growth.

We find that Kamala Markandaya was genuinely concerned with the problems of rural India. Hunger, degradation, population and dowry were the problems most frequently dealt with. Markandaya did it for the sake of amelioration and betterment of the rural folk. Unlike Mulk Raj Anand, Kamala Markandaya does not show any interest in dogmas and propagation of ideas in her novels. Shiv K. Kumar says, "Of all the contemporary Indian novelists writing in English, Kamala Markandaya is the most accomplished, both in respect of her sensitive handling of a foreign medium and her authentic portrayal of the Indian scene. What distinguishes her most incisively from other Indian novelists is her acute awareness of gradual shift in values that has been taking place in this subcontinent."[8]

If we compare the two novelists, we find that Premchand is the son of the soil, while Kamala Markandaya though had knowledge about village life, yet settled outside was always considered as a diasporic and anglicized writer. M.K. Naik feels that Rukmani's village exists only in the expatriate's imagination of her creator. Others feel that she has oversimplified the rural Indian scene of which she is an absent narrator. She is also accused of overplaying poverty in rural India. She did so to make her work acceptable to the western readers. In fact the novel of Markandaya can claim for many strong points. It follows a linear pattern and story extends from one generation to the next, from Nathan's marriage to his death. As William Walse puts it, "She is preoccupied with the opposition between a cerebral, Western—and she seems to be suggesting, a narrowly Benthamite-habit of mind and the more inclusive. Her expatriate status should not be held against her for it allows her the required detachment and objectivity to deal with her subject. The work shares significantly the concerns expressed by Leavis and Thomson's understanding of 'The Organic Community' and the 'The Loss of the Organic Community', of course without nostalgia."[9]

Premchand also talks about the Landlord's point of view and his life and his problems while Kamala Markandaya concentrated only on the problems of landless farmers and their lives. Kamala Markandaya talks about devastating effect of industrialization on farmers, prostitution, dowry and other related social evils. Premchand's description of village life is more realistic. Kamala's characters talk in the language and tone that does not belong to them, sometimes even they sound artificial. Premchand's characters are rooted in their soil and speak the native language, hence more effective. Nathan has extreme emotional involvement with the soil in which he has sweated for about three decades. And now as an old man he cannot contemplate a life away from his beloved land. Almost same views were expressed by Hori when he talks to Gobar. Hori says, "Does anybody ever give up his ancestral property? Look at us for instance. What do we get out of our land? The return does not even equal an anna's wage per head. A servant with a salary of ten rupees per month is better off than us. But we do not give up our land and go in for a job? Do we?" (16).

All these novels present one common fact that it is the way of life in rural India, which still exists—ridden with caste system, discrimination and differences. The stories go deep into the psyche of the characters and also locate them in social realities of that age. The relevance of the stories in the contemporary world makes them very special because one can easily relate to them irrespective of the fact that they were written in pre-independence era.

Hari Mohan Prasad rightly summed up, "Nectar in a Sieve is a town de force on the peasant's life, their toil, their torture, and their anguish their suffering and above all their tragedy. It has been compared with Pearl Buck's *The Good Earth* and with Bhabani Bhattacharya's *So Many Hungers*, it may even be compared with Premchand's *Godan* and *Rangbhoomi*."[10]

NOTES

1. Charles R. Larson, Introduction, Bombay Tiger by Kamala Markandaya, Penguin Books, India, 2008, p. vi.
2. *Ibid.*, vii.
3. V. Krishna Rao, Continuity and Change in the novels of Kamala Markandaya, Perspective on Kamala Markandaya, Vimal Prakashan, Ghaziabad, 1984, p. 56.
4. E. Nageswara Rao, "The Fertility Motif in Kamala Markandaya's *Nectar in a Seive*", *Indian Literature Since Independence* (ed.) Ayyappa Paniker, New Delhi: Indian Association for English Studies, 1991, p. 7.
5. K.R. Chandrashekaran, "East and West in the novels of Kamala Markandaya", *Critical Essays on Indian writing in English* (ed.) M.K. Naik, S.K. Desai and G.S. Amir, Karnataka University, 1968, pp. 62-63.
6. Kamala Markandaya, p. 98.
7. K. Venkate Reddy, *Major Indian Novelists*, New Delhi: Prestige, 1990, p. 79.
8. William Walse, *Commonwealth Literature*, London: OUP, 1973.
9. Shiv K. Kumar, "Tradition and Change in the Novels of Kamala Markandaya". *Kakatya Journal of English Studies,* 3.1, 1978.
10. Hari Mohan Prasad, "The Quintessence of Kamala Markandaya's Art", Quoted in R.K. Dhawan, New Delhi: Indian Association for English Studies, p. 159.

Note: All the quotes from the books *Godan* and *Nectar in a Sieve* has been taken from the following editions.

Kamala Markandaya, *Nectar in a Sieve*, Delhi: Jaico, 1990 (first published in 1954) All quotations are taken from the 1990 jaico edition.

English translation of *Godan* by Jai Ratan, P. Lal known as Godan—A Novel of Peasant India, Jaico Publishing House, Mumbai.

13

Africa and the Africans in Conrad's *Heart of Darkness* and Achebe's *Things Fall Apart*

Prabin Sinha

Conrad is generally regarded today as one of the greatest writers of fiction in English. F.R. Leaves included him in his great tradition of novelists. Conrad was born in Poland which was practically removed from the map of Europe in a series of 'partitions'. The country had been annexed by Russia from the east, Prussia from the west and Austria from the south. His father, a member of the land owning gentry conspired against his Russian overlords, was arrested and found guilty of subversive activities and exiled. Conrad, the five year old son, was soon to become an orphan as both his parents died as a result of their privations when he was only eleven. Conrad, thus, had an early and bitter experience of the forces of imperialism. Conrad entered the British Merchant navy and travelled to far-flung areas on the globe. Eventually he became a British citizen and settled in Kent. Conrad's novels are said to be ambivalent as regards colonialism and imperialism. Perhaps this could be explained by considering that in Poland he had known the life of a nation subjected to (if not vanquished by) imperialism; but in England he knew the life of a nation at the height of her imperial power, proudly ruling the greatest empire the world had ever known.[1]

Marlow says in *Heart of Darkness,* "The conquest of the earth, which mostly means the taking it away from those who have a different complexion or slightly flatter noses than ourselves, is not a pretty thing when you look into it too much."[2]

Chinua Achebe is considered as a master-artist, writer, theorist and post-colonial thinker. Like Conrad, Achebe was also a product of 'the cross-roads of cultures'. His parents were Igbo Christians, among the earliest in a line of converts to Christianity from the Igbo religion. His European education and Christian Catechism, acknowledged by Achebe to be important influences on himself, allowed him to appreciate the culture of Europe, even while he was in sympathy with his own people in their struggles against European colonialism.

Both Conrad and Achebe have approaches and attitudes which are nuanced because of their experiences in life. However, both retain deep-seated attitudes which could not be erased by either bitter experience in Conrad's case or Western education in Achebe's case. Achebe picks Conrad for special treatment when he indicts Conrad as 'a bloody racist' and *Heart of Darkness* as a novel that projects the image of Africa as "the other world", the antithesis of Europe and therefore of civilization, a place where man's vaunted intelligence and refinement are mocked by triumphant bestiality.[3] Indeed Achebe echoes Edward Said's ideas of Orientalism as a discourse when he asserts that Conrad perpetrated the image of Africa as was being circulated in Europe which had not the slightest touch with reality. Conrad, as a Western 'pilgrim', to use a word from the *Heart of Darkness,* used the stereotypical, hackneyed image of Africa because he could not see beyond the representations that were already rampant in Europe and Achebe is unforgiving in his castigation of Conrad because a writer like Conrad with his *Heart of Darkness* taught and constantly evaluated by serious academics and numbered among the half dozen greatest short novels in English language does more damage than whole libraries of books.

Conrad's *Heart of Darkness* is a text about imperialism. The protagonist Marlow's audience is English and 'in telling the story of his African journey Marlow repeats and confirms

Kurtz's action: restoring Africa to European hegemony by historicizing and narrating its strangeness.[4]

Conrad's Africa and the Africans are those of lore, the representation propagated and repeated by imperialist interests who dehumanized and dehistoricized Africa.

A deconstructive reading of the text of *Heart of Darkness* by Edward Said points out that there are two-world views counterpoised. On the one hand are the "savages" of the dark continent with their savage customs and life and on the other hand is European colonialism and imperialism, equally savage, if not more, reflected in the life and customs followed and adhered to by Kurtz, the man entrusted with the colonial civilizing mission. Kurtz's own savagery in hanging the heads of rebels on poles and making the tribesmen crawl to him was worse than the primitive and ignorant savagery of the inhabitants of the dark "continent". Kurtz's wild savagery makes the simple uncomplicated savagery of the Africans a positive relief.

The narrative in *Heart of Darkness* comes to us through Marlow but his account is given to us through the filter of a second shadowy person. Achebe however says that Conrad's efforts towards drawing a cordon sanitaire between himself and the narrator is wasted and therefore "Conrad seems to me (Achebe) to approve of Marlow, with only minor reservations".[5] Marlow's attitude, the narrator in *Heart of Darkness,* can be taken as the attitudes of Conrad regarding colonialism. While Marlow disapproves of the methods and customs employed by Kurtz, he still considers Kurtz a remarkable man. Marlow's ambivalent attitude towards Kurtz shows Conrad's ambivalence regarding colonialism. Conrad was a man of his times and as such could not go beyond the wisdom of the age which consisted in thinking positively about thc mission of colonialism. Still hc had doubts regarding its methods and customs. Conrad was ahead of his times in some ways and a creature of his times in others. Conrad's genius allowed him to realize that the ever present darkness could be colonized or illuminated but that it had also to be acknowledged as independent. Kurtz and Marlow acknowledge the darkness and are ahead of their times in understanding that "the darkness" has an autonomy of its own and can re-invade and reclaim that which imperialism had taken for its own. "Marlow and Kurtz (and presumably also Conrad) are also creatures of their own time and cannot take the next step forward, which would be to recognize that what they saw, disablingly and disparagingly, as a non-European 'darkness' was in fact a non-European world resisting imperialism so as one day to regain sovereignty and independence".[6]

Conrad wrote his *Heart of Darkness* within the Africanist discourse and Michel Foucault says about discourse that it consists "of anonymous and historical rules, always specific as to time and place, and which for a given period and within a social, economic, geographic or linguistic zone, define the framework within which the enunciative functions are exercised".[7] Achebe says in his essay "An Image of Africa" that Conrad did not originate the image of Africa which we find in his book. It was the dominant image of Africa in the Western imagination and Conrad merely brought the peculiar gifts of his mind to bear on that image. The Africans in *Heart of Darkness* except the ones who had acquired some "culture" from the English like the savage who was fireman, an improved specimen, "howled and leaped and spun and made horrid faces". There are also cannibals, the staple of Africanist discourse. The Africans in the novel are anonymous who emerge from and disappear into the forest capriciously just to plague the Whiteman. They are "pre-historic", that is without history or more precisely excluded from history which is European. They can only yell and shout and make incomprehensible noises as Conrad does not think that they could have a language.

Though Conrad admits a kinship between the Africans and himself, he dissociated himself by relegating the Africans to the "night of the first ages". Imperialist discourses like Africanism and Orientalism are incomplete without mention of women. Even in this short novel, Conrad has provided the staple description of an African woman who along with the fireman is the only African to merit individual treatment. She was "savage and superb, wild eyed and magnificent".[8] She is some kind of a mistress to Kurtz and in this role she stands metaphorically for Africa which too is the possession of Kurtz, the white man. Her character is totally predictable and in this she fulfils a structural necessity of the story—a savage counterpart to the refined European woman who comes at the end of the story, Kurtz's intended.

Achebe became a writer and an incisive one at that because of an uneasy relationship between his two identities—first that of an African of the old culture and second that of an African convert Christian with affiliation to the colonial culture. Achebes disillusionment with the colonial culture made him look back to the culture of his Igbo people and this was the catalyst that made him invent African literature in the post-colonial era. Achebe considered himself one of the party of the White man with his Western education and Christian religion in the initial phase of his life. It was only later, Achebe says, that he realized while reading *Heart of Darkness* that he was one of those savages jumping up and down on the beach. Achebe says, "once that kind of enlightenment comes to you, you realize that someone has to write a different story".[9]

Comparing the perspectives of Conrad and Achebe, the most striking difference lies in the fact that Conrad sets the black indigenous Africans in contrast to the white colonialists while Achebe seeks to define the Africans and their culture by drawing equivalence with the whites and their culture. There are two major reasons for Achebe to seek equivalence. The first is that he is trying to show the West in a language of their own that "Africa did not hear of culture for the first time from Europeans".[10] Secondly Achebe was writing in the language of the Europeans but for the Africans. He wanted to make the culture of the Africans comprehensible to the White populace for which he had to show generic similarities between the culture and practices of the White man and the Africans.

In *Things Fall Apart,* Achebe is constantly establishing equivalences through his choice of words, expressing the Igbo in terms of the European in order to make the first comprehensible to the second. In doing so Achebe achieves his purpose of communicating to the Europeans about the Igbo life and cultures. Western guns and chemicals are made the equivalents of spears and sacrifices and defined under the rubric of "war". The Igbo people wrestle the same as the Europeans, they cook and eat as do the Europeans and they have their own indigenous culture as the Europeans have. What Achebe does by insisting on generic similarities is to show Igbo culture as equivalent to the European culture. *Things Fall Apart* is a novel that defines Igbo people or Africans in terms of the Europeans. What the Igbo people do are the same as what the Europeans do in generic terms though there are dissimilarities when we look into the specific details. As for example, the hero Okonkwo is said to have gained fame by fighting a fierce wrestling battle which is similar to what any European hero would do and thus perfectly comprehensible to an European audience but later Achebe mentions that Okonkwo had wrestled a spirit. Similarly, European money is compared to cowries, the currency of the Igbo tribe.

Conrad's *Heart of Darkness* defines the European by taking Africa and things African as the backdrop and similarly in Achebe's *Things Fall Apart,* the Europeans and their culture are the backdrop which serve as the shadowy other of the Africans. Both books presuppose another in relation to which the people with whom they are primarily concerned are defined.

Conrad's *Heart of Darkness* shows Africa and the Africans from an European point of view which was deficient both factually and morally. Reading Achebe's *Things Fall Apart,* we realize the silences, the omissions and the absences which went to make the established image of Africa and the Africans. Though *Heart of Darkness* is silent or has omitted any mention of African culture, there was indigenous culture and *Things Fall Apart* is concerned with the violent overthrow of indigenous culture and the traumatic encounter between Africa and Europe resulting in the imposition of colonial rule. The central theme of the novel of Achebe is, what happens to the values and the moral order of a community when indigenous institutions collapse in the face of European colonialism.

The racist culture of colonialism had wrought havoc on the African people, especially on a psychological level and Achebe felt that Africans had not fully recovered from the traumatic effects of the confrontation with European culture. Achebe went on to argue that his role as a writer was to help his society regain belief in itself and put away the complexes of years of denigration and self abasement. In a situation in which colonial rule had established its authority by inventing and insisting on the racial inferiority of the Africans. *Things Fall Apart* is a retrospective attempt to understand the origins of the present crisis, that is, the crisis of culture generated from the demise of colonial European Culture.

A commendable point to be noted in Achebe's *Things Fall Apart* is that though the novel presents the colonial experience from an African perspective, it does so without romanticizing the African past. Achebe has an ambiguous stance on the culture of his Igbo community. He represents the heroic past of the Igbo community—Okonkwo, the hero had defeated Amalinze, the cat, in the novel's first paragraph—but he also shows the flip side of that culture in the killing of Ikemefuna in the name of morality and religion at the very hands of the hero. Indeed, Achebe, who had had recourse to alternative values and interpretations of culture with his contact with Christian life, could look at Igbo values and morals with a relative approach. Like Conrad who despite being a prey to colonial rapacity in his native Poland could see the benefits of colonialism from his adopted nation, Achebe could also see the benefits of colonialism despite denouncing its many practices. Nigeria becoming a nation from the unity of petty fiefdoms, for example, being one reward of colonialism and having alternative value system from interaction of African and European cultures being another benefit. Like Conrad, Achebe also has ambiguity in his approach to colonialism. This is the reason why Achebe does not relapse into nativism which is a very appealing option once the repressive colonial power subsides. Several thinkers and leaders who appealed to the heroic past to invoke the masses could not retrace their steps to come back to the real present comprising of hybrid identities and newly independent states and cultures degenerated to fundamentalism.

Achebe's Africans are men with religion, morality, culture, history, and philosophy however, rudimentary. They have their moments of glory as well as times of failing. They are like any other people. Achebe shows in his novel the moral complexities and dualities which the hero encounters and his obliviousness to values other than that he reveres leads to his tragedy. What Achebe shows in his novel is that culture is defined by ambivalence rather than unquestioned authority. This same argument can be furthered to question the essentialising that goes in defining the African and by contrast establishing European superiority.

Both *Heart of Darkness* and *Things Fall Apart* can be better appreciated if we consider them in their respective cultures of which they are the product. *Heart of Darkness* is the product of an imperialist culture that rationalized its appropriation of distant lands through careful construction of binaries like civilization/barbarism, progressive/primitive and so on. Conrad's limitation was that he could not see through the ideology of colonialism which mis/represented Africa and accepted the discourse of Africanism in his representation of Africa and African. On the other hand Achebe's *Things Fall Apart* is a product of the hybrid culture emanating from the fusion of Colonial European and indigenous African culture. Achebe himself found standing on the crossroads of cultures and had developed the ability to live between two opposite worlds thereby giving the impression of the two being one. However, the protagonist in *Things Fall Apart* finds it difficult to live in the world which has been taken over by the "other" structures and he commits suicide. Achebe's novel gives the picture of Africa and Africans as a western educated, enlightened African would depict. The novel represents the African experience and is different from the colonial novel in its structure, language and perspective. While Conrad had a discourse from which he drew his material, Achebe is one of the few who started the discourse of post-colonialism, challenging colonial representations and writing back to the Empire.

NOTES

1. Conrad, Joseph, *Lord Jim* (London: Penguin, 1986), p. 13.
2. Conrad, Joseph, *Heart of Darkness* (London: Penguin, 1973), p. 10.
3. Achebe, Chinua, "An Image of Africa" in *Things Fall Apart,* ed. Tapan Basu (New Delhi: World View Publications, 2003), p. 35.
4. Said, Edward, *Culture and Imperialism* (London: Vintage, 1994), p. 198.
5. Achebe, Chinua, "An Image of Africa" in *Things Fall Apart,* ed. Tapan Basu (New Delhi: World View Publications, 2003), p. 40.
6. Said, Edward, *Culture and Imperialism* (London: Vintage, 1994), p. 33.
7. Merquoir, J.G., *Foucault,* 2nd Ed. (London: Harper Collins, 1991), p. 81.
8. Conrad, Joseph, *Heart of Darkness* (London: Penguin, 1973).
9. *Things Fall Apart,* Ed. Tapan Basu (New Delhi: World View Publications, 2003), p. 67.
10. Achebe, Chinua, "An Image of Africa" in *Things Fall Apart,* Ed. Tapan Basu (New Delhi: World View Publications, 2003), p. 67.

14

Tess and Pecola—Their Tragic Ethos

R.P. Pradhan

Tess and Pecola, the two fictional heroines in Thomas Hardy's *Tess of the D'Urbervilles* and in Toni Morrison's *The Bluest Eye* attract our attention for pursuing a comparative study. In spite of situational differences of the two, their life bears an affinity with regard to the nature of their tragic ethos and human sufferings. Their tragedy becomes grim and ghastly because of their physical tortures, rapes and spiritual anguish and it leads to the terrible extermination of Tess and mental derangement of Pecola.

The tragedy of Pecola and Tess is born out of conflict between individual and society. The individual is pitted against a society which is adverse and hostile. In the case of Pecola it is the white domination against the Black that brings about her tragedy. In the case of Tess it is the aggression of the rising new industrial culture over the peasantry of the Wessex that causes her tragedy. The unfavourable external circumstances are there but their tragedy is also a product of their character. Pecola's ambition of embracing a white standard of beauty and the veiled ambition of the mother of Tess to marry her daughter to a person of noble descent and the murder of Alec by Tess contribute to their tragic end in one way or the other.

To portray the tragedy of a poor black girl Pecola is the main thematic concern of Toni Morrison. The African-American novelist who won Nobel Prize for literature (1993) writes *The Bluest Eye* with autobiographical touches. Though she insists that her novels are not autobiographical yet there are some parallels between descriptions in *The Bluest Eye* and her own life experiences. Her maternal grandparents had migrated from Alabania to Ohio in the North in order to escape racism and poverty. Her father had also left Geogia to escape the vacial violence there. Toni Morrison inherited a legacy of resistance to oppression and exploitation. Love of freedom from white slavery and love of self-expression inspired her for making her self identity and the identity of her class through literature. Circumstances had created a fertile ground for the birth of a new literature of protest and it emerged in the form of African-American literature. It was produced by the oppressed and it indicated the oppressors. Toni Morrison became the leading voice of such literature. In a 1986 interview she explained her point of view, "There were no books about me, I didn't exist in all the literature I had read...this person, this female, this black did not exist...."[1] Therefore, she came out to fill the vacancy. For her the black experience stood at the centre of the national history of America. It was expressed through the context of race, class and gender but she transcends the limit. In broad sense her ultimate aim became the quest for identity, the studies of the relation between the individual and the community, the exposition of the problems of good and evil of love and guilt. The narrative of Pecola needs to be perused in these contexts.

Pecola's pursuit of following white standard of physical beauty brings disastrous consequences in her life. Such idea is essentially racist in origin. The white race has glamourised white skin with blue eyes and blond hair as the symbol of beauty. Those who do not possess all these are taken to be ugly and inferior. Toni Morrison works out the devastating effect of the idea on a poor black family. Pecola's mother Pauline herself is the victim of such notion. She is conscious of deformity in her foot and hopes that some deliverer would straighten it. She copies the hair style of the actress Jean Harlow but soon becomes conscious of her lost tooth which makes her look ugly. Her overvaluation of white beauty results in herself hatred and also in the hatred of her off spring. She regards her daughter Pecola as a "nasty little black bitch".

Pecola is treated as Pariah by her own community. Pecola has heard the popular saying that black is ugly, black is evil and black is devil. On the other hand the white colour which is united with power becomes the symbol of the true, the good and the beautiful. Pecola comes to believe in the inherent superiority of the white and the inherent inferiority of the black. She prays for getting blue eyes that shall make her lovable in society and shall give her rank and honour.

Hardy's vision of human tragedy centres round an innocent and unsophisticated country girl who wages a hard struggle against a cruel fate which is basically neutral and indifferent to human sufferings. The novelist's emphasis is not so much on Tess as a peasant girl suffering under the wheels of industrialism as it is on Tess, the individual who comes into conflict with a villain of wealthy class. The first misfortune in her life results from a pure accident namely the death of the family horse. It robs the family of the means of livelihood. Tess is filled with a sense of guilt because she has been the driver of the horse wagon. She is forced by her mother to seek a job at the estate of a bogus kinsman and falls a prey to his sexual lust. She is haunted by an overpowering sense of sin and looks upon herself as a guilty figure.

Tess comes back from Alec in a state of sheer disgust. Later on a child is born to her and it dies soon. "Sorrow" is the name which Tess gives to her baby. Hardy refers to the baby's death in these words, "So passed away sorrow the undesired—that intrusive creature, that bastard gift of shameless Nature, who respects not the social law; a wait to whom eternal Time had been a matter of days merely...."[2]

Her seed of another tragedy is sown when she becomes a dairy maid for earning her bread and comes into contact with Angel Clare. Both of them fall in love with each other but Tess shuns marriage because she is obsessed with her perpetual sense of past guilt. Angel confesses a moral lapse on his part and she forgives him. She hopes the same kind of treatment and drops a letter of confession about her past seduction but it slips under the rug and does not come to the hands of Angel. Tess marries him under the impression that she has been forgiven. He gets the confession just after marriage and deserts Tess. She becomes the weeping bride of one night. Angel judges her by the code of conventional morality and finds her guilty. He goes abroad and Tess becomes a deserted wife. In the last stage of her life she encounters Alec whose lust is reawakened and he tries to capture her for the second time. She goes on rejecting these advances but fate plays another trick with her. Her father dies and the family is rendered homeless. Besides no reply has come from Angel even after two pathetic letters. Under the pressure of family needs and determined pursuit of Alec and continued indifference of Angel, she surrenders to Alec and becomes his mistress. At last Angel returns to claim her. Feeling that Alec has deceived her by persistently telling her that her husband would never return to her, she stabs Alec and joins with her husband Angel. He welcomes her joyfully but their happiness does not last long. She is hanged and Hardy concludes the novel, "'Justice' was done, and the President of the Immortals, in Aeschylean phrase, had ended his sport with Tess."[3]

Hardy uses the word justice in ironical sense. The hanging of Tess for her murder of Alec is legal justice but it is not moral and spiritual. The use of the word "sport" reminds us of the lines of *King Lear*:

> As flies to wanton boys are we to the gods,
> They kill us for their sport.

In the opinion of Hardy a malicious supernatural power called Fate chases Tess and she is mercilessly hunted down. In spite of the role of the cruel fate, the other causes for the tragedy of Tess are also notable, they are three, villainy of Alec, the tyranny of social conventions embodied in Angel Clare and the rise of industrialism and the accompanying disintegration of English peasantry.

The tragedy of Tess is the tragedy of an innocent woman who has done no harm to anybody at all. Hardy idealizes her and calls her a pure woman. Her forced circumstantial surrender to Alec is physical and not spiritual. She kills her rapist in the end and gives an account of her mental purity. The main culprit is Angel. If he had not abandoned her, there would have been no tragedy in her life. She is "more sinn'd against than sinning."

The act of rape is an integral part of the tragedy of Tess but it is not so in the case of Pecola. The seduction of Tess leaves its after effect and becomes a cause of her regular suffering in one way or the other. Who should be blamed for it, Tess or Alec? According to a few critics the sexual experience of Tess in the wood cannot be called a rape. It is because she did acquiesce in what he did to her. Such attitude would do gross injustice to her. We should take into consideration Hardy's direct or indirect comment in this matter also. Hardy presents Tess as a model of "Pure Woman". Alec is portrayed as an evil and traditional corruptor of women. From this point of view the so-called acquiescence should not be taken as willing surrender of Tess. In the opinion of the novelist her conversation with her mother may be cited in this context:

> You ought to have been more careful if you didn't mean to get him to make you his wife!

"Oh, Mother, my Mother!" cried the agonized girl, turning passionately upon her parent as if her poor heart would break. "How could I be expected to know? I was a child when I left this house four months ago. Why didn't you warn me? Ladies know what to fend hands against because they read novels that tell them of these tricks; but I never had the chance O' learning in that way, and you did not help me!"[4]

Tess' passivity may be attribute to her utter physical exhaustion, her sleepy state and her ignorance of what Alec was trying to do. Her weariness made her incapable of resistance. We have no reason to disbelieve her own words to Alec that she had felt somewhat dazed and had not known his intention till it was too late. Hardy nowhere gives us any indication that Tess was drawn towards Alec and was prove to fleshly temptations. Her late surrender also as referred earlier was under the stress of family needs and other factors.

Tess has bodily been soiled but she remains pure in mind and spirit. Ultimately she kills her rapist and in that way gives an account of her purity. This is why she becomes pure woman in view of Hardy.

Pecola becomes an object of incestuous rape. She becomes pregnant by her father and produces child like Tess. Her entire community becomes hostile and wants the baby to die and the baby dies. Toni Morrison does not condemn the rape as it is done in traditional writing. She wants us to understand the circumstances and Cholly's state of mind which led to the act of rape. For that purpose she refers to cholly's ancestral history of moral degradation. He began life as a homeless child. His father Samson Fuller had run away and his mother had abandoned him on a junk heap when he was four days old. His great aunt Jimmy took him and brought him up till her death. At that time he was only fourteen. Again he was sexually humiliated by two whitemen when he was trying to have sex with a cousin in the open. His marriage to Pauline was full of quarrels and violence. He was bitterly frustrated and had lost all hopes and thus sank into drunkenness. He had failed as a husband and he was also failing as a father. Why did he rape his daughter? His emotions at the time of rape were confused. He came home drunk and found his eleven year old daughter standing "The sequence of his emotions was revulsion, guilt, pity, then love". Why was she not happy? He became conscious of his own helplessness to do anything for her. "What could he do for her—ever? What give her? What say to her? What could a burned-out black man say to the hunched back of his eleven-year-old daughter?" It is in this state of mind that he raped his daughter. Such act of rape was a forbidden and horrifying thing. However, Morrison wants to modify the act of rape because it has been done under a poor and depressive condition. Morrison writes,

> I tell you at the beginning of *The Bluest Eye* on the very first page what happened, but now I want you to go with me and look at this, so when you get to the scene where the father rapes the daughter, which is as awful a thing, I suppose, as can be imagined, by the time you get there it's almost irrelevant because I want you look at him and his love for his daughter and his powerlessness

> to help her pain. By that time his embrace, the rape, is all the gift he has left.[5]

Cholly in his guilt and helplessness wants to show love and give something to her but he is not capable of doing that in a concrete manner. The only thing he thinks he can give her is his manhood. His rape in such condition is love but it appears as violence. As Nellie Mckay suggests, "Within the novel Morrison demonstrates that even with the best intentions, people hurt each other when they are chained to circumstances of poverty and low social status. 'Violence' says Morrison, is a distortion of what, perhaps, we want to do."[6]

The germs of tragedy in both the cases may be traced in motherly factors. Pecola's tragedy begins much before her prayer for blue eyes which are for her a symbol of white beauty. No doubt, she follows the conventional standards of beauty which she has absorbed from consumer society. That surrounds her but a more direct source of her obsession with blue eyes in her mother Pauline. The mother in her younger days had given herself upto the scenes of the movies: "She was never able, after her education in the movies, to look at a face and not assign it some category in the scale of absolute beauty, and the scale was one she absorbed in full from the silver screen."[7] Pecola inherited the two traits of the personality of her mother, the condemnation of her personal feature and the imitation of the white model of beauty. The mother became an ideal servant in a rich white family and aspired to copy the white model. In this way the groundwork of her tragedy is laid in hereditary factors.

The tragic line of Tess also begins from parental factors. It is just a matter of chance that her parents discover their descent from the line of a noble family. John Durbeyfield, the father of Tess regarded himself as an ordinary haggler but one day a parson told him that he was an antiquarian and studied family pedegrees. He had discovered that John Durbeyfield belonged to a noble line of knightly family. The news had an exhilarating effect on the mother of Tess. She began to entertain extravagant hopes. She imagined a bright future for her daughter. She thought that her poverty after the loss of the horse would come to an end as Tess would get a job at the house of Alec and he would also marry her. In that way she instigated her daughter to the house of a supposed distant relative and it is from that place that the tragedy of Tess started and it continued throughout her life.

The question of universality has been of paramount importance in the study of traditional tragedies, it seems worthwhile to put the tragedy of Tess and Pecola on that touchstone. The old tragedies have been generally masculine, the tragedies of Pecola and Tess are feminine. They point to universal sufferings of women in one way or the other. The tragedy of Pecola is not an isolated tragedy, it is the tragedy of her community, it is the tragedy of the black people in America. Similarly the tragedy of Tess is the tragedy of innocent peasantry in the wake of the wave of industrialism. Toni Morrison writes the tragedy of Pecola with reference to race, class and gender in American context but her ultimate focus is the universal problem of the quest of identity, the relation between the individual and the community, the problem of good and evil, love and guilt. Hardy's Tess also faces the same problem of identity in English society.

NOTES

1. Sandi Russell, "It's O.K. to say O.K. (An Interview Essay) in *Critical Essays on Toni Morrison,* ed. Nellie Y. Mckay, 45.
2. Thomas Hardy, *Tess of the D'Urberville.* UBS Publishers and Distributors Ltd., New Delhi, 1993, p. 111.
3. Tess, p. 419.
4. *Ibid.*, p. 98.
5. Barbara Hill Rigney, *The Voices of Toni Morrison* (Columbus: Ohio State University Press, 1991), 32, quoted in *Literature and Its Times,* vol. 4, p. 53.
6. Nellie Mckay, "An Interview with Toni Morrison" in *Toni Morrison: Critical Perspective*, p. 397.
7. *The Bluest Eye*, p. 74.

Contributors

Satendra Kumar is an Assistant Professor and Head, Department of English, Govt. P.G. College, Lansdowne, Pauri Garhwal, Uttarakhand.

Nilanshu Kumar Agarwal is Associate Professor in English at Feroze Gandhi College, Rae Bareli, Uttar Pradesh.

Anurag Kumar is associated with Department of Humanities and Social Sciences at IIT Roorkee, Uttarakhand.

Nagendra Kumar is Associate Professor, in Department of Humanities and Social Sciences, IIT Roorkee, Uttarakhand.

Jaya Kapoor is Assistant Professor in English in the University of Allahabad, Uttar Pradesh.

R.N. Rai is Head, Department of English, BHU, Varanasi, Uttar Pradesh. He has authored several books on Indian English Drama.

Ashutosh Singh is associated with Department of English, BHU, Varanasi, Uttar Pradesh.

Supriya Shukla is Associate Professor and Head, Department of English, V.S.S.D. College, Kanpur, Uttar Pradesh.

Vachaspati Dwivedi is Head, Department of English, S.V.P.G. College, Deoria, Uttar Pradesh.

R.P. Pradhan is an Assistant Professor in Department of English, V.S.S.D. College, Kanpur, Uttar Pradesh. He is co-editor of a transnational journal *Illuminati*.

Gourhari Behera is Associate Professor in Department of English at DDU Gorakhpur University, Gorakhpur, Uttar Pradesh.

Sunita Murmu is Assistant Professor in Department of English at DDU Gorakhpur University, Gorakhpur, Uttar Pradesh.

Rajesh Babu Sharma is Assistant Professor in Dept. of English at University of Lucknow, Lucknow, Uttar Pradesh. He is editor of prestigious journal *Dialogue*.

Rajnath, former Head, Department of English in the University of Allahabad is Chief editor of prestigious journal *Literary Criticism*.

Neeru Tandon is Associate Professor in Department of English at V.S.S.D. College, Kanpur, Uttar Pradesh.

Prabin Sinha is Head, Department of English at D.A.V. College, Gorakhpur, Uttar Pradesh.